P9-DCB-817

The College Student's Research Companion

FOURTH EDITION

Arlene Rodda Quaratiello

Neal-Schuman Publishers, Inc.
New York   London

Published by Neal-Schuman Publishers, Inc.
100 William St., Suite 2004
New York, NY 10038

Copyright © 2007 Neal-Schuman Publishers, Inc.

All rights reserved. Reproduction of this book, in whole or in part, without written permission of the publisher, is prohibited.

Printed and bound in the United States of America.

The paper used in this publication meets the minimum requirements of American National Standard for Information Sciences – Permanence of Paper for Printed Library Materials, ANSI Z39.48–1992.

Library of Congress Cataloging-in-Publication Data

Quaratiello, Arlene Rodda.
   The college student's research companion / Arlene Rodda Quaratiello.—4th ed.
      p. cm.
   Includes bibliographical references and indexes.
   ISBN–13:978–1–55570–588–6 (alk. paper)
   ISBN–10:1–55570–588–X (alk. paper)
   1. Library research—United States. 2. Report writing. I. Title.

Z710.Q37 2007
025.5'24—dc22

                                                    2006102705

I dedicate this fourth edition of
The College Student's Research Companion
to the third addition to my family —
my son Joseph
who loves going to the library.

Contents

List of Figures and Tables

FIGURES

TABLES

Preface

I marvel at the fact that ten years ago, when I wrote the first edition of *The College Student's Research Companion,* mobile phones were the size of police radios, and people did not listen to iPods or instant-message friends. I tackled that first edition not only to demystify the workings of a library, but also to link the time-tested principles of research to both traditional library materials and the growing number of advances in electronic information. I knew from my own experiences, first as a somewhat bewildered college freshman and later as an academic librarian, that all students need an easy-to-use handbook when faced with research challenges today. The purpose of this guide remains the same through all the editions. The advances in technologies have all been completely revised and updated.

This fourth edition will help you learn how to conduct inquiries easily and effectively. As a college student you must understand that this ability is not only a professional prerequisite but also the necessary bottom line to be an information-literate citizen. (Impressing friends with finding the best information on the Web is just a cool advantage!) In many ways researching is in your DNA. Your generation grew up with computers, so you realize that while the Internet drastically transforms the way we do research, it also creates a host of fresh conundrums:

- Is it possible to conduct all the research you need in college from only mastering the use of "Google Search" and "I Feel Lucky" keys?
- Can you just skip learning fundamental research skills and still become a truly savvy information seeker?

- Aren't all libraries —brick-and-mortar or virtual—still a bit daunting to the uninitiated?

Even though the Web may appear to have made things easier, in actuality, the information world continues to grow into a more complicated place. *The College Student's Research Companion* takes you through the process of a research project, step-by-step, starting with how to select an initial topic and taking you all the way through to creating proper citations in the bibliography.

It also is designed to guide you through the ever-increasing maze of resources available. While *The College Student's Research Companion* reflects recent developments, it also upholds the philosophy that information should be judged for what it conveys, not how it is conveyed—in other words, for its content rather than its format. I will show how to use both print and electronic resources effectively. Remember, a truly information-literate person has access to all types of material and can then decide which information tool suits his or her needs best.

ORGANIZATION

- Chapter 1, "Mastering Research Basics," discusses topic selection and provides an overview of research.
- Chapter 2, "Decoding Database Searches," explains how to search all types of databases, including online catalogs, periodical indexes, and Web search engines.
- Chapter 3, "Locating Books," focuses on searching an online catalog for books and then physically finding them on the shelves.
- Chapter 4, "Finding Periodicals," discusses how to find articles using indexes in both electronic and print formats.
- Chapter 5, "Exploring Reference Sources," presents an overview of print and computerized sources.

- Chapter 6, "Selecting Electronic Resources," describes the most popular and current online services so you will be better able to choose appropriate databases.
- Chapter 7, "Navigating the World Wide Web," covers searches, and has been updated to reflect the newest sites and the most up-to-date features.
- Chapter 8, "Preparing a Flawless Bibliography," wraps up the book with a discussion of citations.

All chapters have been completely updated and revised, and all include source evaluation; this edition features chapter-by-chapter exercises for hands-on learning.

Please appreciate that you are not alone if you feel a bit overwhelmed with the task of conducting research effectively by using all the resources and materials that the library has to offer. Throughout the book, I compare the "journey" of research with taking a car trip. Once you know your destination and learn how to read a map, a difficult and frustrating expedition can be become a fun excursion of discovery. I hope you find *The College Student's Research Companion* the right friend to have along for the adventure!

Note for Instructors

I designed this guide to alleviate the frustration of instructional librarians who struggle with "one-shot" lectures. Because of the increasing complexities of information technology, there is barely time to touch upon essential principles in a single class period. For schools fortunate enough to have credit courses in library skills, *The College Student's Research Companion* can serve as a textbook.

By reading selected parts of this book, students can come to library instruction sessions with a common background and make the most of the time available. They will then have the book to refer to once the class is over. This fourth edition makes the job easier with the introduction of exercises in every chapter, which can also be used as discussion-starting questions. The exercises—in an easy-to-print format, along with the answers and other suggestions—are available on a CD-ROM directly from the publisher. For further information, please contact *info@neal-schuman.com* and put "textbook CD-ROM for instructors" in the subject line.

One

Mastering Research Basics

Maria, a freshman majoring in computer science, is taking a required English composition course. She has a paper due in about two weeks that must discuss a controversial issue currently in the news. She has chosen to write about how young adults are using the Web as a social network, and the pros and cons of popular sites such as MySpace.com and Facebook.

Maria goes to the librarian at the reference desk in her college library for help. "I'm writing a research paper about how high school and college students use the Web for socializing. You know, like when you go on MySpace.com and Facebook," she states, then asks, "How can I find stuff about this?" The librarian confidently responds, "That's a pretty new issue, so let's go to the computer and search the online index for articles, and then we can search the catalog to see if any books have been published yet."

Another student, Nils, who is in the same class, reluctantly goes to the library two weeks later (the night before his paper is due) and hesitantly goes to the reference desk after wandering around the library aimlessly for some time. "Um . . . I don't know how to use the library," he admits, "but I have a paper due tomorrow and I can't find anything . . . I tried surfing the Web in my dorm room but that was a waste of time. Where are the books about controversial issues? My professor says I need scholarly articles too."

The librarian asks, "I can't help you very much until you've chosen a topic. Do you have any ideas?"

Which student do you think will have more success in doing research and a more pleasant library experience? It's hard to picture Nils having a very good time in the library. His classmate Maria will not only have a better experience, she will probably get a better grade too.

CHOOSING YOUR RESEARCH DESTINATION

Many students walk into the library with a research assignment and no idea what to do next. These are the students who become confused and overwhelmed by the idea of doing research because they don't really know what they're looking for in the first place. The first thing you should do to avoid frustration in the library is to clarify with your professor anything you don't understand about the assignment. Then you need to come up with a topic you can be enthusiastic about.

The most crucial step in the research process is defining what you're looking for, just as you first choose a destination when planning a trip. This step is necessary to give you a firm foundation. Maria and Nils have been given the same assignment: to write a research paper on a current controversial issue. Maria has selected a narrow topic to write about, probably something that holds some personal interest for her because it relates to her chosen major. She has a clear idea of where she's headed. Nils hasn't nailed down a topic yet, and so he has no idea what information he really needs. He thinks that if he goes to the library and browses, he'll find what he needs. But he's probably going to have a difficult time, especially since he's starting the night before the paper is due.

When selecting a topic, it's always wise to choose something that will engage your curiosity—something that will motivate you when the going gets rough. When you plan a trip, for example, you naturally are drawn toward a place that appeals to you. In the same way, pick a paper topic that appeals to you. Think about the discussions in your classes that were interesting, something that you heard on the news that you would like to pursue further, or just something of personal interest. Brainstorm ideas with your friends and classmates.

Even if you're not given a great deal of latitude in choosing a topic for a particular class assignment, you can come up with a "twist" that will make researching the assigned topic interesting. Relate it to something that does interest you. For instance, Maria in the previous example is really interested in computers. She's taking the English composition class because it's required. So she relates the given assignment to computers—particularly, to the use of the Web.

For another example, let's say that you're taking a required World Civilization course and have to do a paper about some aspect of ancient Greek civilization. Unless you're a history or classics major, this assignment probably doesn't sound too thrilling at first. But perhaps you are interested in sports. You could study the ancient Olympic Games and the role that sport played in Greek society.

If you are stuck, there are a variety of Web sites that can help you think strategically about topic selection. Purdue University's Online Writing Lab (OWL) is especially useful, providing a wide range of instructive approaches to the problem. Topic: Invention Techniques, a particularly useful page, can be found online at: http://owl.english.purdue.edu/workshops/hypertext/ResearchW/invent.html. Also valuable is Planning (Invention): Thought Starters, which can be found at: http://owl.english.purdue.edu/handouts/general/gl_plan3.html. It is also important to remember that, while you may need a topic to get your research started, the topic may change as you go ahead with your project. Things that you learn along the way may transform your expectations and interests.

Once you feel that you have zoomed in on an interesting subject, write down a brief statement of your topic. Next, write down the major research questions that you'll want to answer. Like a journalist, ask yourself, "Who, what, why, where, when, and how?" To continue with our example, here are just a few questions Maria will need to address:

- Who uses MySpace.com and Facebook and other social networking sites?
- Why do people use these sites?
- What are the pros and cons of using these sites or having a personal Web site?
- How do these sites work?
- How else do young adults use the Web as a social network?

If you can write such a list of questions, you'll have a clear understanding of your needs. The process of writing them down will also make your destination more concrete.

You don't have to pinpoint your topic to the minutest detail. In fact, if you're too narrow in your selection, you will limit yourself. Finding that balance between too broad and too narrow is an art that is often mastered through trial and error. You may find that once you start your research, your original topic will evolve into something different from what you had imagined. Something you come across in your reading may take you down another road. But such detours don't have to take you out of your way—in fact, they often take you on a shortcut to your ultimate goal.

Just remember, if you have no idea where you're going, you'll probably never get there. This fact holds true on the road as well as in the library.

PLANNING YOUR RESEARCH TRIP

Why should you have a plan? Well, without one, you'll probably end up wasting precious time browsing through the library. So after you've determined your topic, you should map out your route by:

- identifying the types of sources that will provide you with the information you need
- determining where and how you will find these sources
- estimating how much time you will need to do your research

Although browsing can be effective in the preliminary phase of research by helping you select a topic and perhaps find some general information, it's not a very good method to use once you've chosen a topic—especially if your topic is very narrow. So think of browsing as a joyride—you have no particular destination but you may see some interesting things along the way. There's nothing wrong with browsing. It's actually a great way to learn. But some students go to the library the day before a paper is due and try to get information by surfing the Web, flipping through issues of magazines, or wandering through a section of the library that seems to have books relating to their subjects. This usually doesn't work very well.

Types of Sources

Books

Despite the prevalence of computers and electronic resources, books are probably what first comes to mind when you think of a library, and books do make up the bulk of just about all library collections. There are two main types of books in the library: circulating books (those you can check out) and reference books (those you must use within the library). These collections are generally kept in two separate areas of the building and are arranged by Library of Congress or Dewey Decimal call numbers. Some libraries also put selected books (such as those useful to a particular class) on special reserve, allowing them to be checked out under particular circumstances or for finite amounts of time.
    Although a growing number of students seem to have de-

veloped an aversion to books and prefer to rely on the World Wide Web, books provide a depth of coverage that is hard to beat. It is important to remember that authors can pay to have their books published by vanity presses, so the simple fact that a text is bound does not always mean that the writer is an expert in what he or she is discussing. Even so, most books printed by reputable publishers must go through a rigorous editorial process before being published. Facts must be checked and sources of information confirmed. While anyone can publish on the Web, authors of non-vanity books must possess some expertise to have a book published. So if you want to gain a thorough knowledge of your topic, you must check to see if there are any relevant books. If you are uncertain about the text's value, see what you can figure out about the author's credentials. You can also look up the publisher, determine what other books it has published, and examine its editorial policy.

If you're still uncomfortable about the prospect of using books in your research, remember that you don't have to read these books cover to cover. Maybe there's just one pertinent chapter. Review the table of contents and index to determine which parts of a book to focus on. Your goal should be to find the best information for your project, and books are often the best way to go about getting that information.

Traditional ideas about what constitutes a book are certainly changing as an increasing number of books in print are also published in electronic format. Often reference sources like encyclopedias, dictionaries, and handbooks, which are useful for obtaining quick and concise factual information on a broad range of topics, are available electronically. A Web site called Xreferplus (www.xreferplus.com), for example, provides online versions of hundreds of reference sources. Classic works that are no longer restricted by copyright and so are considered to be in the "public domain" (such as the Bible or *Moby-Dick*) have been available via Project Gutenberg (http://promo.net/pg) since the early days of the Internet. Another commercial site, eBooks (www.

ebooks.com), contains nearly 70,000 titles. Many colleges subscribe to a Web-based resource called NetLibrary (www.netlibrary.com) which provides the full text of over 100,000 books, still merely a sampling of the books that have been published. On Amazon.com (www.amazon.com) you can now search inside many books; this feature can help you determine whether particular books will be useful. Google Books (http://books.google.com) provides a similar service, allowing you to input a word or phrase and determine books in which it appears.

According to the Library of Congress Web site (www.loc.gov/about), there are 29 million books contained in the collections of this massive national library. Considering this fact, it becomes clear that only a small number of sources originally published in book form are available via the Web. You should not rely solely on electronic books since printed books still make up the vast majority of a library's collection. Don't choose a book simply because it is available electronically.

Periodical Articles

Finding articles in periodicals is another essential component of doing research. Periodicals include all publications that come out on an ongoing basis, including magazines and journals. As with books, there is generally some sort of editorial process that gives the material added validity. It is generally hard to get a magazine to accept an article, and it is even harder to get a journal to do so. As any writer will tell you, it's easy to have an article rejected from a periodical, and it often takes a good deal of persistence to get published.

Types of periodicals include:

- newspapers
- popular magazines
- scholarly journals

The difference between popular magazines and scholarly

journals will be discussed at greater length in Chapter 4. Although students often confuse the two terms and tend to use them interchangeably, the main difference is that when your professors require you to use journal articles rather than those in magazines, they mean you should find publications of a more scholarly nature. The word "magazine" usually indicates a publication of a lighter sort for a more general audience, while the word "journal" is more often used when referring to an academic source, but the distinction can be blurry. Sometimes periodicals provide the only useful information on very narrow or very current topics.

Web-Based Resources

The Web includes two types of information: sources that were originally published in print and sources unique to the Web. Periodical articles that you can obtain through Web-based indexes or electronic books available from subscription services like NetLibrary should not be confused with Web sites that have no print equivalent. There are also an increasing number of Web-based periodicals, such as the online magazine *Slate* (www.slate.com), which is owned by the *Washington Post.*

While evaluating the information you find in book and periodical sources remains important, evaluating Web-based material is even more crucial. As mentioned before, anyone can put anything on the Web, and sites often lack depth, authority, and accuracy. Although there is a great deal of interesting material available on the Web and it can be a good source of quick information, proceed with caution.

Of course, a library provides more than just books, periodicals, and Web access. There are many other types of informational resources, such as videotapes and DVDs, government documents, conference papers, dissertations, maps, and photos. Many libraries also have special collections that may relate in some way to the college curriculum or local history. These resources often can't be pigeonholed into the broad categories above. Sometimes there is overlap, and you will find references to these kinds of items while searching for books, periodicals, and Web sites. For example, some libraries include nonbook material in their online catalogs, while government documents are covered in various indexes.

How and Where to Find Sources

Once you have pinpointed your informational needs, you'll require the means to fulfill these needs—just as you'd need a car to get to your destination. To do effective research, you have to know how to use the traditional library as well as the virtual one. In addition to knowing the basics of how libraries are organized, you will find it helpful to utilize online catalogs, electronic indexes, and Web search engines. All of these resources can be defined as databases, and Chapter 2 will explain how you search a database to find the information you need.

Chapter 3 will explain how to use an online catalog most efficiently to find books and other library material on your topic. From the catalog, you obtain titles and call numbers. This information is essential if you want to get your hands on the items described in the catalog, and so is an understanding of the organizational system (either Dewey Decimal or the Library of Congress classification) at your library.

To find articles in periodicals, you don't just browse through issues of magazines or journals or surf the Web, hoping to find the complete text of an article on your topic. You first need to select the appropriate indexes, the vast majority of which are available online. Each index covers a different set of periodicals. Some indexes cover broad ranges of subjects, and others focus on more narrow disciplines. Often there is a lot of overlap, and there are many indexes from which to choose. You should become familiar with those available in your library and determine the most appropriate ones to find articles pertaining to your topic.

To find Web sites, you must know how Web search engines work. Surfing the Web, like browsing in the library, can be very ineffective. Just as online catalogs enable you to find books, and periodical indexes help you find articles, search engines locate Web sites. The problem is that when you use these tools, which are far from perfect, you often find a lot of irrelevant material. This problem is due partly to the amount of junk that is on the Web, partly to ineffective use of the search engines, and partly to the design of the tools themselves. You can never be quite sure what you're going to find. Although you can't control the content of the Web or the way the search engines work, you can learn to use them as effectively as possible.

Learning how to use all these resources isn't something you want to do right before a paper is due. You didn't learn how to drive a car for one particular trip. You learned to drive so that you would have a practical skill for life. In this information society, finding information is also a skill you must develop to be successful in life, so you should become familiar with the library even before your first assignment is given. Even if you don't have a particular project yet, stop by the library and get acquainted with it and with the helpful staff who work there. Explore the various electronic resources, even if you can't try all of them. Practice using your library's computers by looking up a subject of personal interest. What's your favorite TV show? Look it up in the electronic indexes and see what critics have to say about it. Where would you like to go for spring break? See if the library has any books about this destination.

Don't be shy about asking librarians for help. Their job is to assist you with any questions you have, and your tuition pays their salaries, so take advantage of their services. Go on a tour if one is being offered, even if you think it might be a bore—you'll be glad you did later, even if all you remember is the location of the most comfortable study space. If you are given the opportunity to go with one of your classes to an instructional session, don't choose that day to cut class—you'll be sorry when the rest of your classmates breeze through their research. Finally, of course, read the rest of this book. The time you invest now in learning how to navigate through the library will save you a great deal of frustration in the future.

Using Other Libraries

Planning your route will also involve decisions such as whether to use the resources of another library. Since not every library can buy every book or provide access to every periodical source, you may have to go elsewhere for the material you need, particularly if another college library has a special collection that relates to your subject. Many smaller academic libraries have limited budgets and select books based on the academic programs of the school. A college that specializes in technology will have a lot of science books, but maybe not such a great collection in literature and the fine arts. Your library might be a member of a consortium— a group of libraries in the same area that share resources. You can also get materials that you need through interlibrary loan (ILL), a service available at just about every library, which locates a hard-to-find book or article elsewhere in the country and delivers it to your library. This is a helpful service, but you have to allow at least a week or two for the material to arrive. In some cases it can take as few as two or three days, but don't depend on it at the last minute.

Planning Your Time

Although waiting until the last minute is a common practice, you should expect to be particularly stressed if you do this. The research process is time-consuming, no matter how many time-saving hints I give you. Another important aspect of the planning stage is determining how long you will need to do your research and complete your paper.

There are two phases to completing a research paper: doing

the research and writing the paper. Too often, students dismiss the research process as that boring task they have to get over with in the beginning. Research is a major component of a research paper; that's why it's called a *research* paper, and why I've written an entire book about doing research papers that focuses on research rather than on writing. Without information, you have nothing to write about. Good research results in papers that will get high marks from your professors.

Although computers are a tremendous aid, they don't just spit out the exact information you need without some mental effort on your part. And you usually can't get all the information you need on a computer screen. Although an increasing number of computer databases provide the text of articles on screen, and complete electronic versions of many books are available on the Web, you'll most likely only get your hands on some of the material you need by acquiring paper copies. This process requires time and effort.

The length of the paper as well as your own research experience will, of course, determine when you should start your research. The University of Minnesota Library has an "Assignment Calculator" on its Web site (www.lib.umn.edu/ help/calculator) which attempts to break down the process of writing a research paper into manageable steps. Just enter the date you plan to start your research and the date the paper is due, and the calculator will respond with a day-by-day guide to the steps you should be taking, including selecting a topic; finding and evaluating books, articles, and Web sites; and writing a first draft. According to this calculator, research should take about half of your time.

Allow yourself time for roadblocks along the way—a book you need has been checked out, you realize that you'll have to go to another library or get a book through interlibrary loan, the computer system has crashed—there are any number of scenarios. Sometimes your gut instincts tell you when it's time to start. A mild anxiety may come over you.

Since the cure for worry is action, just getting started will make you feel better.

Set aside a short time for an initial visit to the library well in advance of your paper's due date. Promise yourself you'll spend an hour on your research, but don't put any pressure on yourself. You don't even have to be successful in finding anything. Just go. Chances are you will have positive results. Then go again the next day. Spend some time each day working on your research. Take small steps and you'll see that slowly everything will come together. This method really works—in fact, it's the approach I took in completing this book.

If you're stuck, it can also be helpful to visit your library's Web site or even to stop by the library itself. The wide variety of resources that libraries make available may well jump-start your imagination.

ABOUT THE EXAMPLES USED IN THIS BOOK

The car in which you learned to drive may not be the car you drive now. But because all cars operate according to the same principles, you'll find that things are fundamentally the same: you put your foot on the gas pedal to make the car accelerate or on the brake to slow down or stop, you turn the wheel to steer. Sure, little things are different: on a dark night when it starts to rain and you're borrowing a friend's car, you may have to search frantically for the windshield wiper controls or defroster. In the future, perhaps, as you sit behind the wheel of your new hydrogen-powered SUV complete with DVD-player and GPS navigation system, you might look upon the car you drove in driver's ed as an antique, but the lessons you learned in that gas-powered vehicle should still be easily transferable.

The examples used in this book can be like that driver's ed car. Although you may not use exactly the same resources in your library, the examples I have chosen demonstrate fundamental principles that will enable you to use the particular resources that are at your disposal.

It is unavoidable that the sources I cover in the rapidly changing world of information technology will undergo minor as well as drastic modifications by the time you read this book. But I believe that most of these changes will be superficial, just as the look and performance of cars have been altered over the years but the way you drive them hasn't changed much. That's why it's so important to understand the basic theories of doing research rather than the specifics. Computers are constantly being upgraded and—supposedly—improved, but this trend leaves the average user feeling confused and a bit intimidated. The examples in this book, on the contrary, will demonstrate the fundamentals that endure, rather than give you specific instructions that might change before this book is even published. With the knowledge of the underlying theories, you will have a road map that will lead you through unfamiliar territory.

Consider the Research Road Less Traveled

U.S. Route 66 was the first highway constructed between Chicago and California back in the 1920s. It remained the major east-west route until the superhighway Interstate 40 was built parallel to it in the 1970s. Now Route 66 has become a byway, a back road that is traveled by tourists who have time to sightsee rather than by drivers who are in a hurry to get somewhere. With all its roadside pit stops, hamburger joints, neon signs, teepees, ghost towns, and other quirky attractions, Route 66 is a much more interesting road to travel than Interstate 40, which looks like just about every other superhighway in America. Tourists come from all over the world to "get [their] kicks on Route 66."

Similarly, computerized resources have paved a superhighway through our libraries. Traditional resources remain but are often overlooked. Computers have certainly revolutionized the library. Electronic periodical indexes, multimedia reference sources, and the World Wide Web have changed the way research is done, in countless ways. Some of these changes are good but others are not. The main problem that has arisen with the emergence of computerized resources is that many students have come to rely exclusively on computers. These students ask, "Why read a book?" and "Why track down old journal articles on microfilm?" Why limit yourself? There is still plenty of information that is not available electronically and may never be.

You should choose your resources based on content rather than format; in other words, judge a resource on its informational value rather than on whether it's readily available. As you read this book and utilize the techniques discussed in it, keep in mind that the best resources might not be the easiest to get. It may take you a little more time to find that obscure journal article or book, but it may well be worth it. Remember what Robert Frost wrote: "Two roads diverged in a wood, and I—I took the one less traveled by, and that has made all the difference."

EXERCISES

Using a particular research assignment answer the following questions:

1) What topic have you chosen? Write a brief statement:

   _____

   _____

2) Briefly list five major research questions that you will need to answer:

   • _____ ?
   • _____ ?
   • _____ ?
   • _____ ?
   • _____ ?

3) Listed below are the various types of resources that are found in a library or via a library Web site. Rank them according to how useful you think that type of resource will be for finding information on your topic (1 being the most useful):

   ___ newspaper articles
   ___ books
   ___ scholarly journal articles
   ___ Web sites
   ___ reference sources
   ___ magazine articles
   ___ other material (maps, DVDs, and so on); specify:

   _____

4) Name three other libraries in your area that might be helpful for your research:

   • _____
   • _____
   • _____

Two

Decoding Database Searches

The time has come, like when you got behind the wheel for your first driving lesson, to start working on your research paper. Whether you go to a computer workstation at the library or use your own computer in your dorm room or a laptop in the dining hall, your journey begins with a visit to your library's Web site. Library sites each have a unique look, but fundamentally they provide the same types of resources. In addition to information regarding the library and its services, there should be a link to the online catalog, which provides information about all the items that the library owns. Another link should provide access to the electronic databases, including periodical indexes and reference sources that the library subscribes to.

THE STRUCTURE OF DATABASES

Many of the resources that are available through library Web sites can generally be described as databases. A 'database' is basically a collection of information in computerized format. The online catalog, for example, is a collection of information about the items owned by a particular library. Each item owned by your library, whether it be a book, a journal, a DVD, or something else, has a 'record' in your library's online catalog. Figure 2.1 is an example of a record for a book.

Author: *Friedman*, Thomas L.
Title: The world is *flat* : a brief history of the twenty-first century / Thomas L. *Friedman*.
Link to Internet Site: Table of contents
Edition: 1st ed.
Publisher: New York : Farrar, Straus and Giroux, 2005.
Subject Heading(s): Diffusion of innovations.
Information society.
Globalization Economic aspects.
Globalization Social aspects.
Description: viii, 488 p. ; 24 cm.
Notes: Includes index.
Contents: Part I. How the world become *flat*. While I was sleeping -- The ten forces that flattened the world -- The triple convergence -- The great sorting out. Part II. America and the *flat* world. America and free trade -- The untouchables -- The quiet crisis -- This is not a test. Part III. Developing countries and the *flat* world. The Virgin of Guadalupe. Part IV. Companies and the *flat* world. How companies cope. Part V. Geopolitics and the *flat* world. The unflat world -- The Dell theory of conflict prevention. Part VI. Conclusion : imagination. 11/9 versus 9/11.
ISBN: 0374292884 (hardcover : alk. paper)

Figure 2.1: An example of an online catalog record.

Just as a database is composed of individual records, each record is composed of individual elements, called fields. A 'field' is a certain type of information about the item. Fields in a record for a book include:

- author, title, and publication information
- physical description—the number of pages, as well as the book's length and height
- subject headings and sometimes the table of contents (The example in Figure 2.1 lists the contents and also has a Web link to the table of contents.)
- notes indicating such things as whether the book has an index
- numbers that identify the book, such as the International Standard Book Number (ISBN)[*] or the Library of Congress Control Number (LCCN)

---

[*]   The ISBN in Figure 2.1 is the old ten-digit variety. As of

The record will also indicate the library where the item is located, its call number (much more about this in Chapter 3), and the status, indicating whether the book is available or checked out.

Another type of database that is commonly available on library Web sites is the electronic periodical index—a collection of records describing articles in magazines and journals. Figure 2.2 displays a record from an index for a journal article.

A record for an article is generally comprised of the following fields:

- article title (or headline, in the case of a newspaper article)
- author
- periodical title (sometimes referred to as the source) along with the issue, volume, date, and page numbers needed to locate the article
- subject headings or terms (also commonly referred to as descriptors). Specialized subject headings such as geographic terms or people may also be included.
- abstract (a summary of the article)
- text (if available). Some databases designate a separate field for the lead paragraph of an article. This practice is helpful for searching purposes, because if your keywords appear in the first paragraph, it is likely that they are not just passing references; therefore the articles retrieved when searching the lead paragraph will be more relevant than those found searching the entire article.

Other databases that may be available on a library Web site are electronic versions of reference sources, including encyclopedias, dictionaries, and almanacs. Many of these sources will be discussed in Chapter 5.

January 2007, ISBNs now have 13 digits. Any books written before 2007 can be identified by the prefix 978 followed by the original ten-digit number.

Title:	**The Revenge of Mrs. Santa Claus or *Martha Stewart* Does Christmas.**
Authors:	Marling, Karal Ann
Source:	American Studies; Summer2001, Vol. 42 Issue 2, p133, 6p
Document Type:	Article
Subject Terms:	*CHRISTMAS
Geographic Terms:	UNITED States
People:	STEWART, Martha
Abstract:	Focuses on the views of the author concerning the ideal christmas of *Martha Stewart* in the United States. Accounts on the pleasure during the festive season; Ignorance on the quality of cigar; Celebration of christmas of material culture through material culture of all sorts.
ISSN:	0026-3079

Find More Like This

Figure 2.2: An example of a record from EBSCOhost Academic Search.

Computerized resources have many advantages over traditional resources in print. Since multiple volumes of an index, an encyclopedia, or some other type of reference source can be stored in a single database, you are saved the time of repeating your search in each volume of a print source. Computerized indexes require much less physical space than printed indexes, and they often include abstracts and other supplementary material. Another advantage is that you don't have to copy citations by hand; instead, you can print out any pertinent information that you find, or you can download records or e-mail them to yourself. It's also much easier to search a computerized resource because you can use keywords. On the other hand, keep in mind that online indexes vary greatly in the range of dates that they cover, in their user friendliness, and in the kinds of searching that they allow. Thus, while computerized indexes are extremely useful, you should not rule out the value of the print variety.

SEARCHING A DATABASE

Databases can be composed of thousands, sometimes even millions of records. How do you find the records that pertain to your topic out of this huge amount of information? By utilizing the searching techniques described in this section, you will save lots of time and frustration. There are two basic ways of finding information on a topic: by keyword and by subject. Keywords are words that appear anywhere in a database record while subjects are the standard terms under which items are categorized. The full range of a keyword search actually varies from one index to the next, so be sure you figure out what kind of results you're likely to get from such an operation before you decide to rely on it. A subject search will only locate words in the subject field. Although it is more precise to find a book or article by subject, keyword searching is a good way to start your search.

Keywords and Boolean Logic

Keyword searching allows you to search for single words or phrases, as well as combinations of words and phrases, in just about any field. As a general rule, it is best to avoid using common prepositions and articles (such as 'the,' 'of,' 'to'), called stop words, as well as three special terms, 'and,' 'or,' and 'not,' which serve a special function to be discussed shortly. The principles discussed here are extremely important because they form the basis of searching any computerized database and of using Web search engines effectively.

Keep in mind that different databases employ Boolean operators in different ways. Some include the operators as part of their search interface. Others, like Google, simply insert the AND operator (discussed below) between words.

Using the Connector AND

Unless you have a very general topic that can be defined by a single word or phrase, you need to know how to do a keyword search for multiple keywords. Keyword searching is invaluable for finding material on multidisciplinary subjects that are difficult if not impossible to define by one single subject. Keyword searching using more than one term or phrase operates according to the principles of Boolean logic, which were developed by George Boole, a 19th-century mathematician. These principles are quite straightforward. Boolean logic can be used to define a topic very specifically, so that from among millions of records in a database you can find the ones that meet your needs.

Suppose you wanted articles about drug abuse among women. To understand Boolean logic, picture two sets of articles: the first contains all those about women, and the second contains all those about drug abuse. The articles that are about both women and drug abuse form a common subset. When the search **women and drug abuse** is entered,

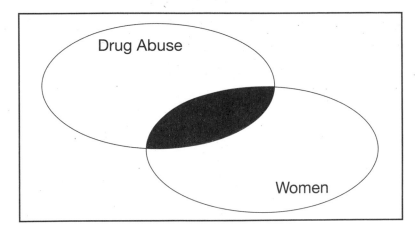

Figure 2.3: Diagram representing a search for **women and drug abuse**.

records that contain the two terms specified are retrieved, as illustrated in Figure 2.3.

The portion of this diagram in black is the set representing records that include the terms **women** and **drug abuse**. The more terms you link together, the narrower your search becomes and the fewer records you will retrieve. For instance, a search for **women and drug abuse and treatment** will retrieve a narrower set, as in Figure 2.4.

The portion of this diagram in black is the set representing records that include the terms **women** and **drug abuse** and **treatment**. Notice that it is smaller than the highlighted portion in Figure 2.3.

If you don't find any records, or if you only find a few, you can try dropping a term. This will broaden your search. Or, if you get too much, narrow your search by adding a term. You will find that keyword searching can often be a process of trial and error, like finding your way around an unfamiliar area without a map.

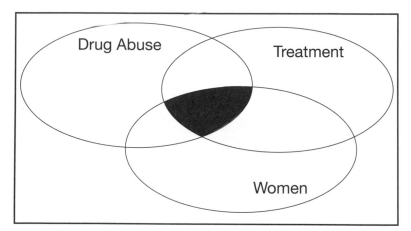

Figure 2.4: Diagram representing a search for **women and drug abuse and treatment**.

Using the Connector OR

You can also use the word OR between terms to broaden a keyword search. Picture a set containing all the books about air pollution and another set containing all the books about water pollution. Some of these books may certainly overlap in subject material covering both topics. But the set resulting from a search for **air pollution or water pollution** will contain not only the books that address both topics but also those that are about one topic or the other.

In Figure 2.5, the area in black represents those books that address both topics, but the areas in gray are also included in the resultant set because the connecting term OR was used. If you were to add another term to this search using OR, the outcome would be even larger because the more terms you link together with OR, the broader your search becomes; this is the opposite of what happens when using AND.

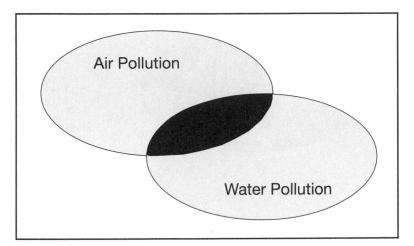

Figure 2.5: Diagram representing a search for **air pollution or water pollution**.

Truncation

Truncation can serve a purpose similar to that of OR. With this technique, available in many databases, you drop the ending of a word and replace it with a truncation symbol. This symbol differs among catalogs and other computerized databases. The question mark (?), asterisk (*), and pound signs (#) are frequently used. For example, you could enter **environment?**, which would retrieve all of the records containing any words beginning with 'environment'; in addition to 'environment' itself, you would also retrieve 'environments,' 'environmental,' 'environmentalists,' and so on. Occasionally no symbol is necessary and truncation is automatic. If you're uncertain, be sure to check the database's online help files regarding truncation and wild card searching before you get going.

Truncation is helpful when you want to retrieve both the plural and singular forms of a word; just substitute the truncation symbol for the 's.' In some databases you can also

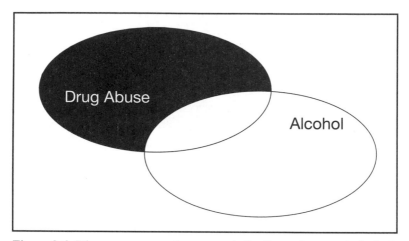

Figure 2.6: Diagram representing a search for **drug abuse not alcohol**.

use truncation symbols within words. For instance, if you wanted to find either **woman** or **women**, you might be able to enter **wom?n** which would serve the same purpose as the lengthier **woman or women**.

Using the Connector NOT

You can use the word NOT between terms to eliminate ir-relevant items. For example, if you wanted to find all the articles about drug abuse in a particular periodical index but weren't interested in those dealing with alcohol, you could enter the search as **drug abuse not alcohol**. This would eliminate all the records in which the word 'alcohol' appears, as Figure 2.6 illustrates.

In this figure, the area in black again represents the re-sultant set. Now, though, it is a subset not of both original sets, but only of the set of books about drug abuse. Although NOT is used less often than the other two connecting terms, it can be very helpful in avoiding one of the pitfalls of key-word searching—retrieving irrelevant records.

Combining Connectors

You can combine ANDs, ORs, and NOTs in one search to get really specific. Although my examples here will involve using parentheses, many Web-based catalogs simplify the process with advanced search entry forms that provide lots of boxes in which to enter terms and pull-down menus to select the appropriate connecting term. What's important to understand is the theory behind this technique of combining search terms. Using parentheses when combining sets, or entering search terms separately in the boxes on a search form define your search criteria so the system or database can sort terms out according to the rules it uses to search. Check the online help to find out what these rules are.

For example:

> **(drug abuse not alcohol) and women**
> retrieves records concerning drug abuse among women but not alcohol abuse

> **children and violence and (motion pictures or television)**
> retrieves records about the effects of violence in both movies and TV on children

If I searched the library catalog for **drug abuse not (alcohol and women)** instead of **(drug abuse not alcohol) and women**, I wouldn't find any books on women because the *not* eliminates both words inside the parentheses. **(Children and violence and motion pictures) or television** will retrieve books about children and movie violence as well as *every* book in the library about TV whether or not it has anything to do with children and violence.

Problems with Keyword Searching

Although keyword searching can allow you to search a database with great precision, it does have disadvantages. The first problem is a lack of comprehensiveness. Keyword searching does not necessarily retrieve every record on a subject. For example, if you were to search EBSCOhost Academic Search Premier for articles about bird flu and look up **bird flu** as a keyword phrase, you would find a lot of records that contain this phrase. Most of these records will list **avian influenza** as a subject heading. Not every record for an article with the subject heading **avian influenza**, however, will contain the keyword phrase **bird flu,** since that's not the official name of the disease. If you look up **avian influenza**, you will retrieve twice as many records for this topic than if you search for **bird flu**.

Another drawback is the retrieval of irrelevant material. Keyword searching often retrieves irrelevant material because it takes words out of context. If you wanted a book about the architecture of Boston and were to enter **boston and architecture** in the online catalog, in addition to retrieving all the records for books about Boston architecture, you would also retrieve all the books about architecture that were published in Boston but not necessarily about Boston. Remember that basic keyword searching generally picks up words throughout the record, including the publisher field.

Finally, keyword searching often retrieves peripheral material. Because keyword searching searches throughout the item record that might also include summaries for books or even the full text of articles, you might also get a lot of records that will contain only a small amount of information on your topic.

Field-Specific Searching

To lessen the possibility of retrieving irrelevant or peripheral material, some databases allow you to limit your keyword searches to particular fields in a record. For example, for books about Boston architecture, you could indicate that you only want these words located within the subject headings of records or within the titles. This would eliminate books that were published in Boston but not about Boston. Limiting keyword searches to subjects and titles is an excellent way to refine your search if you find that you have retrieved too many records or irrelevant records. This method will be discussed in more detail in Chapter 4.

Searching by Subject

Despite the apparent ease of keyword searching, there is no better way to retrieve a complete list of relevant material than by subject searching. Although finding the appropriate subject heading is often a process of trial and error, it's worth the effort. Some search engines, such as Yahoo!, do have subject directories, but we can only hope that someday there will be a system for subject searching the Web as thorough as those currently used for online catalogs and periodical indexes. We'll discuss subject searching in more detail later in the book, but part of the reason you retrieve so much junk when using Web search engines to find Web sites is that the Web does not rely on subject headings in its overall organization.

Most database records have a subject field. In the online catalog, books are assigned Library of Congress Subject Headings (LCSH) so there is a standard terminology used by all libraries to categorize their books. Chapter 3 will describe in greater detail how to determine the proper subject headings when searching the online catalog for books. Unfortunately, there are no universal subject headings used to classify articles as there are for books. Although some online services have adopted LC headings, many periodical databases have their own terminology. Some databases have special names for the subject heading field: for example, PsycINFO has descriptors and MEDLINE has MESH (medical subject headings). Thus subject searching for specific topics can often be problematic.

One way to determine appropriate subject headings both in online catalogs and periodical indexes is to do a keyword search first and then click on the subject headings of the pertinent books or articles that you retrieve. This procedure will lead you to all the records categorized under a particular heading. Web-based databases simplify this process because subject headings are usually Web links. For example, if you do a keyword search for **athletes and steroids** in an online catalog, you'll probably retrieve some records that list **doping in sports** as a subject heading. Simply click on this heading to find all the books in the library about this subject.

To perform a subject search directly, you may need to go to an advanced search screen or select a subject search option from a pull-down menu. Although most databases provide a subject searching option, it may not be on the first screen you see because often the default search method is keyword searching.

Unless you're really into cars, you don't know how to deal with every mechanical problem. But it's good to know some of the basics like changing a tire. In the same way, don't feel that you have to become an expert at searching every database. It's more practical to focus on one database—preferably the one that will cover the majority of your research needs, such as Expanded Academic ASAP or Academic Search. When the need arises for you to use another, more specific, database, you can always ask a librarian for help, just as you can go to a mechanic when your car is in need of repair.

Evaluating Your Sources: The PACAC Method—Overview

Doing research is not just about finding information, it's also about evaluating what you've found and determining what will be useful. Evaluating your sources is an ongoing process. With the constantly increasing amount of information available and the powerful electronic tools we now have for accessing it, you may well discover, to your surprise and dismay, that you're overwhelmed with too many resources. Don't select a source for the sake of adding one more item to your bibliography. The quality of your information is more important than the quantity.

Evaluation focuses on five main characteristics: purpose, authority, content, accuracy, and currency (just remember PACAC). This focus is important for books, articles, Web sites—any information. At the end of each subsequent chapter, one of these PACAC characteristics will be highlighted. When evaluating sources, disregard the format. A source should be judged for what it contains, not how it is stored. Remember that the most useful sources for your research may not always be the easiest material to get your hands on. You might have to go to microfilm to get an old newspaper article or use a print index to find articles from the pre-computer days. Although you should appreciate the information superhighway that has been created by computers, you should also see the value of the informational "back roads."

EXERCISES

1) Keyword searching often requires you to think of synonyms. For example, what are three other terms that you might include in your search if you want to find all the records in a particular database about **teenagers**? _____ OR _____ OR _____

2) Which of the following is another way of expressing a Boolean search for air pollution or water pollution:

   a) air or water pollution
   b) (air or water) and pollution
   c) air and water and pollution
   d) air pollution or water

3) You would like to find articles about Ireland's World Cup soccer team but you keep finding records for the United Kingdom team which includes Northern Ireland. Which of the following searches would allow you to eliminate the unwanted information:

   a) ireland not (northern and soccer)
   b) ireland and (soccer not northern)
   c) (ireland and soccer) not northern
   d) soccer not northern ireland

4) Insert the Boolean connecting term that is most likely to make the following search phrases find books about Native Americans:
   Indians _____ America
   Indians _____ India
   (North America _____ South America) _____ Indians

Answers: 1) adolescents OR high school students OR young adults; 2) b; 3) c; 4) AND; NOT; OR, AND

Three

Locating Books

Despite the changing times, books are still usually the first thing you associate with libraries. To find the books that you need from among all the thousands of books in the library, you need to use the online catalog. You also use the online catalog to find other material besides books, such as periodicals, CDs, DVDs, and videotapes. Since the vast majority of online catalogs are now available via the Web, searching them is similar to searching any computerized database, whether it be a periodical index for finding articles or a Web search engine for finding Web sites.

Because you will probably need to search the catalogs of other libraries at some time, which can easily be done on the Web, it is useful to understand the basics that underlie all systems. The catalog of another library may be just a mouse-click away. There is also the possibility—especially if you're at a small school—that your library is part of a consortium and shares its catalog with other libraries in the area.

SEARCHING THE ONLINE CATALOG

Although the layout and format of the online catalogs of different libraries may vary, fundamentally they all operate in the same way. There are four basic ways of finding books: by title, by author, by subject, and by keyword. Figure 3.1

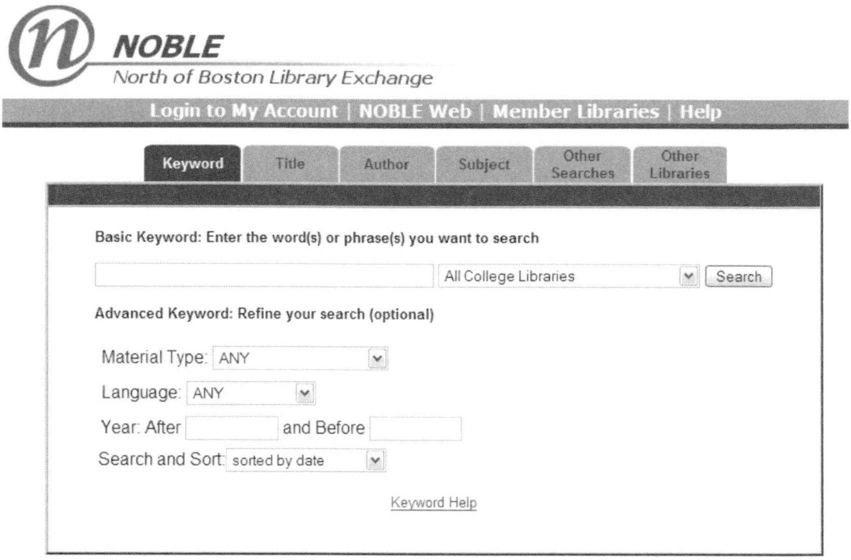

Figure 3.1: An example of an online catalog's opening search screen.

displays a sample opening Web page for an online catalog. By clicking on the link that specifies the type of search you want to do, you will access the appropriate form for entering your search criteria. Many online catalogs, including this one, make their default search a keyword search. Unless you choose another search option, the first form to appear will be a keyword form. Aside from the four basic searches, there is usually an option like Other Searches that allows you to perform advanced searches or searches by numbers such as call number or ISBN (International Standard Book Number). Online catalogs such as this one often allow you to limit your search (in this case using pull-down menus) by:

- library where items are located if your library is a member of a consortium
- type of material—books or nonbooks
- language—most useful for eliminating foreign language works
- date of publication

Searching by Title or Author

It's easy to find a book if you know the author's name or the exact title. Just a couple of simple rules are commonly used when searching for books by author or title:

- When looking up an author, use the last name first. Example: **king stephen** (usually no comma is necessary and all lowercase is fine)

- When looking up a title, the general rule is to drop any articles (although many catalogs will now just ignore 'a,' 'an,' and 'the'). Example: *A Tale of Two Cities* should be entered **tale of two cities**

If you do not find what you're looking for, first make sure that you have followed these two rules, then check to make sure that you have the correct spelling and that the author or title you have entered is a valid one. The computer cannot read your mind; contrary to popular belief, it is just a stupid machine that takes all the commands you give it quite literally.

Searching by Subject

Here's an example of searching the online catalog by subject. Let's say you are doing a paper on bioterrorism. Your first inclination would probably be to enter the subject heading **bioterrorism**. If you do this, you will certainly find books if your library has any on the topic. After clicking on the search button, you will see subject headings similar to those listed on the screen displayed in Figure 3.2.

The first heading, **Bioterrorism—See also the narrower term Agroterrorism**, is actually a cross-reference. Cross-references are often narrower topics that fall under the main subject area, but they can also stand alone. If you clicked on **Agroterrorism** you would go to a screen that would list

SUBJECTS (1–12 of 29)	Year	Entries 158 Found
Bioterrorism -- See Also the narrower term Agroterrorism		1
Bioterrorism		9
Bioterrorism Computer Simulation	c2004	1
Bioterrorism Electronic Information Resources		2
Bioterrorism Government Policy United States		17
Bioterrorism Health Aspects	2003	1
Bioterrorism Health Aspects Study And Teaching United States	2003	1
Bioterrorism Health Aspects United States		6
Bioterrorism Juvenile Literature	2003	1
Bioterrorism Law And Legislation -- See Bioterrorism		1
Bioterrorism Popular Works		3
Bioterrorism Prevention		6

Figure 3.2: An example of a subject heading list in an online catalog.

titles of any items pertaining to that subject. Below the cross-reference link is the main heading **Bioterrorism**, which is followed by subheadings such as **Computer Simulation** and **Prevention**. These are also narrower topics under the main heading, but they subdivide the main heading and cannot stand alone. At this level, years of publication are only included for subject headings that have one item.

Once you have found the appropriate subject heading, you are not finished because your goal is to get your hands on some books on the topic. You must delve to the next level to find the individual book records by clicking on the heading you want. Clicking on the main heading **Bioterrorism** brings up a list of the individual books and other items, as shown in Figure 3.3.

This screen simply lists titles and authors. If you want to see the complete records you need to click on a particular title. You should take a look at some of the full records because most books are assigned more than one subject heading. You will notice in Figure 3.4 that the book has two other subject headings in addition to **Bioterrorism**. These subjects may be related to your research topic, so you might be interested in following them further. You can easily do this using a Web-based catalog. Simply click on the subject heading. By clicking the link for **Smallpox—History**, you will instantly retrieve the records for all the books on this subject. This is a powerful feature that gives you the ability to explore related material in a convenient manner.

Subject searching doesn't always work as effortlessly as the previous example might suggest. Sure, **Bioterrorism** is a subject heading, but not everything you might think to enter is going to be a heading. It's the same as when you look up a listing in the yellow pages and find that doctors aren't listed under **Doctors** but under **Physicians**. Subject headings are determined by the Library of Congress, which puts together the official list of standard, acceptable headings under which all library material is categorized. The print version of the list is actually quite long, contained in five

Title		Date
Biological Weapons Defense : Infectious Diseases And Counterbioterrorism / edited By Luther E. Lindler, Frank J. Lebeda, George W. Korch ; Forewords By David R. Franz, Matthew See FULL RECORD for availability details.		c2005
Biological Weapons : From The Invention Of State-Sponsored Programs To Contemporary Bioterrorism / Jeanne Guillemin See FULL RECORD for availability details.		c2005
Bioterrorism A Clear And Present Danger / [Electronic Resource] : Anthony S. Fauci ; Introduced By James A. Thomson See FULL RECORD for availability details.		2003
Bioterrorism : Guidelines For Medical And Public Health Management / Donald A. Henderson, Thomas V. Inglesby, Tara O'Toole See FULL RECORD for availability details.		c2002
Fire Department Response To Biological Threat At B'nai B'rith Headquarters, Washington, DC, April 19 / [Electronic Resource] / [Investigated By Jeff Stern] See FULL RECORD for availability details.		1997?
The Gathering Biological Warfare Storm / [Electronic Resource] / Jim A. Davis, Barry R. Schneider, Editors See FULL RECORD for availability details.		2002
The Life And Death Of Smallpox / Ian And Jenifer Glynn See FULL RECORD for availability details.		2004
Safe Food : Bacteria, Biotechnology, And Bioterrorism / Marion Nestle See FULL RECORD for availability details.		c2003
Terrorist Threats To The United States : Hearing Before The Special Oversight Panel On Terrorism Of The Committee On Armed Services, House Of Representatives, One Hundred Sixth Congress, Second Session, Hearing Held May 23, 2000 See FULL RECORD for availability details.		2000

Figure 3.3: A typical online catalog title display.

Record 7 of 9

Record: Previous Next

Author	Glynn, Ian
Title	**The life and death of smallpox / Ian and Jenifer Glynn**
Imprint	New York : Cambridge University Press, 2004

LOCATION	CALL #	STATUS
Dimond - Level 5	RC183.1 .G49 2004	AVAILABLE
Manchester General Coll	RC183.1 .G49 2004	AVAILABLE

Description	x, 278 p. : ill. ; 24 cm
Bibliography	Includes bibliographical references (p. 246-268) and index
Subject	Smallpox -- History
	Smallpox -- Vaccination -- History
	Bioterrorism
Author ae	Glynn, Jenifer
ISBN	0521845424

Figure 3.4: An individual book record in an online catalog.

big red books known as *Library of Congress Subject Headings*, LCSH, or, simply, the 'red books.'

If you took the time to leaf through the pages of the 'red books,' they would certainly help you determine appropriate headings to enter in the online catalog. But let's be realistic—you probably won't want to look through such a massive work while you're searching the online catalog. You could take a look at a Web-based version available from Mississippi State University (http://fantasia.cse.msstate.edu/lcshdb/index.cgi). But it's also useful to review the structure of the print list even if you don't ever use it, because it will give you a better understanding of how subject headings work.

In this alphabetically arranged list, official headings are indicated by bold type. **Television advertising** is one such heading, as displayed in Figure 3.5.

What does all this mean?

UF (use for)—terms that **Television advertising** should be used for. This part isn't too useful, basically telling you, for example, that **Television advertising** should be used instead of **Television commercials**. Conversely, however, if you had looked up **Television commercials**, you would have been told to **USE Television advertising**—this is helpful.

BT (broader term)—terms that will retrieve more material or material that covers a broader subject area. For example, **Broadcast advertising** will find material that covers advertising on both television and radio, so you'll probably find more books, or books that have a wider scope of information, if you use that term.

RT (related term)—suggestions for other terms you could try. In this example, **Television commercial films** is a related term.

NT (narrower term)—terms that will limit your search. If you look up **Cable television advertising** or **Singing commercials**, which are narrower, more specialized subjects, you will find fewer books.

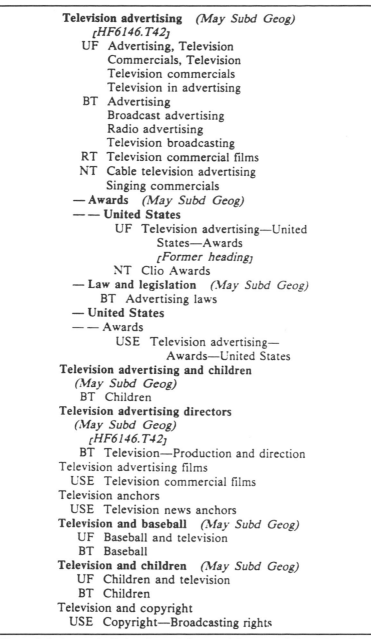

Television advertising *(May Subd Geog)*
  ₍HF6146.T42₎
  UF Advertising, Television
     Commercials, Television
     Television commercials
     Television in advertising
  BT Advertising
     Broadcast advertising
     Radio advertising
     Television broadcasting
  RT Television commercial films
  NT Cable television advertising
     Singing commercials
  — **Awards** *(May Subd Geog)*
  — — **United States**
       UF Television advertising—United
          States—Awards
          ₍Former heading₎
     NT Clio Awards
  — **Law and legislation** *(May Subd Geog)*
     BT Advertising laws
  — **United States**
  — — Awards
       USE Television advertising—
          Awards—United States
Television advertising and children
  (May Subd Geog)
  BT Children
Television advertising directors
  (May Subd Geog)
    ₍HF6146.T42₎
  BT Television—Production and direction
Television advertising films
  USE Television commercial films
Television anchors
  USE Television news anchors
Television and baseball *(May Subd Geog)*
  UF Baseball and television
  BT Baseball
Television and children *(May Subd Geog)*
  UF Children and television
  BT Children
Television and copyright
  USE Copyright—Broadcasting rights

Figure 3.5: A sample listing from *Library of Congress Subject Headings*.

Below all these terms begins the list of subheadings you can use with **Television advertising**, which includes **Awards** and **Law and legislation** and **United States**.

The online catalog will often perform the same function as the 'red books,' referring you to official headings as well as associated headings. Let's say you were looking for books about Native American tribes. You'd probably just enter the subject heading **Native Americans**. Having done this, however, you would see the following reference in the catalog: "'Native Americans' is not used in this library's catalog. **Indians of North America** is used instead." In a Web catalog, cross-references are links to other Web pages, so you could just click on **Indians of North America** and easily perform the right search.

The wheels of the Library of Congress, as with any large bureaucratic institution, move slowly. Headings do change to reflect the times. **Moving picture plays**, for instance, was eventually changed to **Motion pictures** and **Baby busters** to **Generation X**, but you are less likely to find terms in current usage established as subject headings. **Web logs**, the official term for 'blogs' was only recently added to the list. For new words like 'blogs' that are not yet official subjects, it is best to employ a keyword search first, using it to determine the relevant subject headings.

Sometimes subject searching can be downright infuriating. If you entered **War in Iraq**, which is not a subject heading, you would be informed that there are no books on this subject. Often just changing the word order or playing around with the phrase a bit will do the trick. For example, you will find that **Iraq War** is a valid heading.

Another suggestion is to think of synonyms for your heading. Perhaps, considering the formality of Library of Congress subject headings, you might think to enter **Daytime dramas** to find books on soap operas, when, in fact, the official heading *is* **Soap operas,** despite the colloquial sound of that term.

Searching by Keyword

Suppose you are looking for books about headhunters (the kind that can get you a job, not the kind you often see on reruns of that classic 1960s sitcom *Gilligan's Island*). If you perform a subject search, you will find books about both varieties of headhunters. But *My Friends, the New Guinea Headhunters* won't help you with your career. *How to Answer a Headhunter's Call: A Complete Guide to Executive Search* may. Since the subject heading under which this book is officially categorized is **Executives—recruiting**, doing a traditional subject search would never have located it, but this keyword search does. You can do this sort of thing with an online catalog or just about any other searchable electronic database.

All of the principles of Boolean logic discussed in Chapter 2 apply to searching the online catalog. Suppose, for example, you can't remember the exact title of a particular book or the author's name but you know some of the words. You know that the author's first name is Ann and the word 'pants' is in the title. By entering the keyword search **ann and pants**, you are able to locate *The Sisterhood of the Traveling Pants* by Ann Brashares. Pretty cool, don't you think?

UNDERSTANDING THE CLASSIFICATION SYSTEMS

Using the library can be a lot like navigating a new city. Say you were looking for a particular address on your first visit to New York City. When you first got off the subway, you might feel overwhelmed by the buildings, crowds, and noise. It might be hard to see any order in all the chaos. Luckily, most of Manhattan is laid out on a grid, and the streets are numbered in order from south to north and east to west. Once you understand this, navigating becomes a breeze.

Libraries can be compared to Manhattan. Although they are usually much quieter, they can be big and often overwhelming. When students go into them, they often think it will be hard to find their way around. But finding the book you need is easy once you learn the system. Libraries these days certainly contain much more than just books, but books still take up the most space, and books are often what you look for when you begin your research. The average college library contains hundreds of thousands of books; a large university library contains millions! Even if your library contains millions of books, you can easily find what you need amid this overwhelming amount of material if you understand how everything is organized. With this understanding, you will also be able to locate periodicals, videos, and other nonbook material in the many libraries that organize these collections in the same way as their book collections.

There really weren't too many libraries before the 19th century, except for those catering to the needs of academic institutions or individuals who could afford to pay dues. Each one of these private libraries organized its books in a different way. But in the 1800s, several factors—all related to the Industrial Revolution—led to the rise of libraries. A more technologically literate society was needed to support the rise of industry, so public education and literacy became widespread. At the same time, technological advances in printing, which transformed it from a manual to a mechanical process, made the production of books less expensive and easier. Finally, Andrew Carnegie and other leaders of industry donated large sums of money to support the building of new libraries. With more books, more people reading them, and more libraries, there was a greater need for a standard system of organization. Two systems actually emerged: Dewey Decimal Classification, used in many public libraries and some smaller college libraries, and Library of Congress (LC) Classification, the standard in larger public institutions and most academic libraries.

In order to get your hands on the books you have identified in the online catalog, you need to be familiar with either the Library of Congress system or, less frequently, the Dewey Decimal System, depending on which is used by your library. Students usually have trouble finding books on the shelves because they don't really understand the system that is used to arrange them. There are probably countless students who don't ask library staff for help, but instead just wander through the shelves wasting precious time and getting frustrated. To avoid getting lost, consider the following crash course in how libraries arrange books on the shelves (or, 'in the stacks').

Libraries give call numbers to books in order to classify them by subject and author. This method groups books on similar topics together on library bookshelves. You find out a book's call number by looking it up in the library's online catalog. With Dewey call numbers as well as the LC call numbers, the subject matter and the author's name determine the number a book is given, which in turn determines its location on the shelf.

Dewey Decimal Classification

Dewey Decimal Classification divides knowledge into ten broad categories, from the 000s through the 900s. Each broad category is subdivided into ten more sections, which are each further subdivided into ten smaller sections and so on until you get down to the level of individual books that will have call numbers involving decimals. For example, if you are interested in literature, the books you want are located between 800 and 899. More specifically, books of American literature are between 810 and 819. This section is further subdivided into such sections as poetry, drama, and essays, each designated by a whole number. Nineteenth-century American writers are primarily found within the 818 section. Although individual libraries may differ slightly in the exact call numbers they assign to their books, a copy of Henry David Thoreau's classic *Walden* might have the spe-

Table 3.1 Dewey Decimal Classification.

000–099   **General Works**—like encyclopedias, but a lot of other topics have been thrown in over the years ranging from Bigfoot and UFOs to computers and the Internet.

100–199   **Philosophy**—this also includes psychology, astrology, witchcraft, and related topics.

200–299   **Religion**—200–289 includes Christianity, while all other world religions are crammed into the 290-299 section.

300–399   **Social science**—includes sociology, political science, economics, and related topics.

400–499   **Languages**—here you will find books about individual languages as well as linguistics in general.

500–599   **Natural sciences** (as opposed to applied sciences, which are covered in the next section)— books on mathematics, astronomy, chemistry, physics, and life sciences are found here.

600–699   **Technology**—includes applied sciences ranging from medicine and engineering to cooking.

700–799   **Fine arts**—includes painting, sculpture, music, performing arts, television, games, and the like.

800–899   **Literature**—includes classic literary works as well as literary criticism, but does not usually include contemporary fiction and other works not considered "classic" (these are generally kept in a separate fiction section arranged by author).

900–999   **History**—in addition to historical topics, includes biographies which are all kept in the 920 section.

cific call number 818.3. To summarize this sample hierar-chical scheme:

800–899 Literature
  810–819 American literature
    818 Nineteenth-century American literature
    818.3 Thoreau's *Walden*

The part of the number following the decimal point can be a bit confusing. Just to review some basic math, decimals don't have the same value as whole numbers. For instance, *Walden*, as well as books about *Walden*, at 818.3 will actu-ally be found to the right of a book with a number like 818.298, because .3 is greater than .298. When using deci-mals, zeros get dropped, so .3 is really the same as .30 or .300 and so on to infinity. When zeros are appended, it's easier to see that .300 is greater than .298.

Dewey Decimal Classification has some inherent weak-nesses. Its hierarchical scheme has a strong bias toward Western culture as well as a lack of concern for political cor-rectness. A similar situation is obvious with the emphasis on American, British, and Western European literature. The lit-erature of countries that were considered alien to most people in 19th-century America—Asian, African, and Middle Eastern countries, as well as Russia, Poland, and many others—is squeezed between 890 and 899.

Another problem with this system is that, as new subjects arise, they must be shoehorned in somewhere. The original 19th-century scheme had no place for such topics as com-puter programming and television, so computer books are commonly thrown in with the encyclopedias, and you'll usu-ally find the books about television along with all the books on movies in the fine arts section, specifically 791.4 (not even a whole number!). Because of this problem, books in these and other unforeseen areas must have long and com-plicated call numbers in order to give each a unique location.

Library of Congress Classification

Library of Congress Classification is more complex. It is used by some larger public libraries, many academic libraries, and, of course, by the Library of Congress, which designed it in the 19th century to organize the increasing number of books in its collection. This national library has grown from a one-room legal collection established in the Capitol in 1802 for the use of Congress to a massive institution that contains over 100 million items. Such a vast collection requires a more specific scheme of organization; Dewey Decimals are not sufficient for the task.

The LC system breaks all of knowledge down into 20 broad categories indicated by letters of the alphabet (see Table 3.2). You'll find encyclopedias in the A section, atlases in the G section, and literature in the P section. You may think it's odd that Military and Naval Science are considered top-level categories, but you have to remember that the original purpose of the scheme was to serve the needs of the government. The basic categories are subdivided alphabetically. For example, while books on literature are given the letter P, English literature is PR and American literature is PS.

The LC system is alphanumeric. Following the initial one-, two-, or occasionally three-letter code are numbers that further divide a particular topic. If you're looking for humor (which you may be needing if you've gotten this far in the chapter), go to the PN6160 area. In many libraries, Ellen Degeneres's *The Funny Thing Is . . .* has the call number PN6165 .D44. How would you go about getting your hands on this item? Locating the book on the shelf is akin to locating a particular building in New York City, since the books are all shelved in a certain order. But the Library of Congress system is more complicated than this analogy implies because, like the Dewey Decimal Classification System, it also utilizes decimal points as well as an often confusing jumble of letters and numbers. It's more like finding the building and *then* finding a particular suite.

Table 3.2 Library of Congress Classification.

A   **General works** such as encyclopedias.

B   **Philosophy**, **religion**, and **psychology**.

C   **History**—special topics like archaeology, geneology, and general biography.

D   **World history**.

E/F **American** and **Canadian history**.

G   **Geography** (mostly)—in addition to atlases and books about various geographic areas, you'll also find books about such unrelated topics as the environment, dancing, and sports.

H   **Social sciences**—includes sociology, economics, and business.

J   **Political sciences**.

K   **Law**.

L   **Education**.

M   **Music**.

N   **Fine arts**—includes painting, sculpture, and architecture.

P   **Literature**—also includes theater, movies, and television.

Q   **Natural sciences**—mathematics, astronomy, chemistry, physics, life sciences, and so on.

R   **Medicine**.

S   **Agriculture**.

T   **Technology**—other applied sciences like engineering, photography, and cooking.

U   **Military science**.

V   **Naval science**.

Z   **Bibliography**—library science as well as bibliographies that list materials on various subjects.

So you want to get a copy of *The Funny Thing Is . . .* at PN6165 .D44. Here are the steps to take:

- First, you have to find out where the P section is located. Consult a floor chart or ask your friendly librarian.
- Once you find the general P section, finding the PN area is simply a matter of alphabetical order—it will be between the PMs and the POs.
- When you find the PN area, follow the call numbers numerically until you get to 6165. Be sure that the number you look for is six-*thousand* one-*hundred* sixty-five and not six-hundred sixteen point five. If you try looking for PN616.5, you'll wind up in a totally different section from PN6165 and you'll see books about ancient literature—certainly not what you had in mind.
- Once you have found PN6165, switch back to the alphabet to find D (which stands for the author's last name).
- After finding the D section, you encounter the trickiest part of the LC Classification: the dreaded decimals. You need to look for .44 (just drop the D now that you've found it). Recalling our discussion of decimals earlier in the chapter, would *The Funny Thing Is . . .* at PN6165 .D44 be found before or after the book *How to Be a Superhero* by 'Dr. Metroplis' at PN6165 .D7? Is .7 less than .44? No, because .7 is the same as .70, which is greater than .44. So Ellen's book comes before the "doctor's." At first glance, you might think that these books would actually go in the opposite order, but if you just mentally insert some zeros, it becomes clear that this is the proper arrangement.

The year of publication is often included at the end of the call number, but I have omitted it here so the numbers appear a bit less daunting. This date is only important in distinguishing one edition of a book from another.

In reality, what often happens is this: you find the general section you need, such as PN6165, and then, realizing that the books in this section are arranged by author's last name, simply scan the titles on the shelf to find what you need rather than straining your eyes looking at those little call numbers on the book spines. This method can work effectively in many situations.

Library of Congress call numbers, however, are not always as simple as in the humor section. As mentioned before, when classification systems were developed in the 19th century, many subjects did not even exist. So when books about such topics as airplanes, television, and space tourism were written, they had to be fit in somewhere. As a result, a lot of books have been crammed into very small call number ranges and therefore must have very long call numbers with lots of digits, letters, and decimals.

For example, let's take a look at the section of the library that contains books about the Internet. Although 15 years ago you would have found few books about the Internet in most libraries, now there are thousands of titles in print, and all of them are usually designated by call numbers starting with TK5105.875 .I57. *The Complete Idiot's Pocket Reference to the Internet* has the lengthy call number TK5105.875 .I57 G65. If you break down this call number, it's really not too much harder to find than *The Funny Thing Is . . .* ; it just looks more intimidating.

- After finding TK, and then 5105, look for TK 5105.875 the way you look for any decimal.
- Then you find .I57 by first locating the TK 5105.875 books that begin with the letter I on the next line after the call number. Next, look for the TK 5105.875 I books with .57 after the letter I.
- Finally, after finding G (which stands for Goldman, the author's last name), you regard 65 as a decimal also, even though there's no decimal point before the G. In the LC scheme, any number after the initial whole number is regarded as a decimal. So *The Internet for Windows* by David C. Gardner at TK5105.875 .I57 G368 will be shelved to the left of TK5105.875 .I57 G65.

There is another confusing aspect of the LC Classification. Where's the fiction section? Libraries that use LC numbers usually don't have a separate fiction section as do public libraries using Dewey Decimals. This is because the LC scheme is intended more for research than for recreational purposes. Fiction is most often put in the literature section (designated by call numbers beginning with P), side by side with criticism of the various works. The same is true for biographical material: Dewey libraries tend to put most biographies in the 920s, whereas LC libraries have them scattered throughout the collection, depending on the occupation of the person about whom the book is written.

Many books are hard to classify because they might involve more than one subject. A book about the psychology of women, for example, may be classified in the HQ section rather than BF, which is the primary psychology section, because HQ contains books on women's studies. Depending on how you look at the book, it could fit in either section. If this book on the psychology of women was of a more medical nature, it could even be placed in the RCs. If there's only one copy of the book, however, it can only have one distinct call number, so the librarian who catalogs the book must make a choice. The same problem can occur when a book is classified with the Dewey Decimal system. This is why it is important to use the online catalog rather than just meandering through the stacks; you may find that books on basically the same subject are in different call number areas.

Once you get familiar with the system used to organize books, however, you can do some 'educated browsing.' Although browsing can be an effective way to do research, if you practice 'educated browsing' in certain call number areas, you often serendipitously find some useful material. Of course, if you're looking for something really narrow, you may have problems. Restrict your browsing to more general information on a topic. To be an 'educated browser,' look up your subject in the online catalog and find a few relevant books and their call numbers. Then, after locating these books in the stacks, take a look at what other books are on the shelf nearby.

As a side note, another way to find further material once you're in the stacks and have found a few books is to look in the back of each of these books for a bibliography of sources. If you notice any titles in the bibliography that look pertinent, look them up in the online catalog to see if your library has them.

Although both the Library of Congress and Dewey Decimal classification systems were developed in the 19th century, these two systems still serve to give some order to what could easily be chaos. There are even some Web directories that organize Web sites based on these schemes. A growing number of libraries are organizing Web resources using the same classification schemes that have been used for years to organize more traditional resources. The designer of CyberDewey, David A. Mundie (who is not a librarian), describes his site, which has been around for over a decade, as "A Hotlist of Internet Sites organized using Dewey Decimal Classification codes," and explains why these traditional classification systems still deserve our attention: "It became clear that library classifications were ideally suited to my organizational needs. They have evolved over a long period of time to solve exactly the sorts of problems that confronted me, and they embody a tremendous amount of collective wisdom."[1]

---

[1]   David A. Mundie, "Organizing Computer Resources," CyberDewey, 1995. <www.anthus.com/CyberDewey/Organizing_computers.html> (3/12/07).

Evaluating Your Sources: The PACAC Method—Purpose

WHY IS THE INFORMATION BEING PROVIDED?

Determining a writer's intent is important when evaluating your sources, especially when it comes to Web sites, but also applies to any informational resources. Ask yourself if a particular resource is intended to promote a product, cause, or organization or if its only purpose is to provide information. An encyclopedia article, for example, is written primarily to convey factual information. Although an online version of an encyclopedia may display advertising on the Web page, the content of the articles is generally unbiased. Other resources may serve ulterior purposes. Perhaps a magazine article is written to promote a particular cause. The author of a book can also promote a certain viewpoint. Reference sources, either in print or online, tend to be the most unbiased resources, while free Web sites must be evaluated for purpose with the most caution. Obviously, the purpose of any source that is offered without charge is not to make money. There must be another reason for its existence. Although this reason could be the desire of the writer to share information freely, more likely it is not so magnanimous. This is why it is best to consult Web resources that your library subscribes to before searching the rest of the Web.

EXERCISES

1) List two Library of Congress subject headings that would locate material on your current paper topic:

   _____

   _____

2) Choosing one of the main headings you listed above, indicate one subheading and one related heading that would also be helpful in your research:

   subheading: _____

   related heading: _____

3) Put the following call numbers in the order you would find the corresponding books on a library shelf, 1 being the first and so on:

   a)
   ____ RC514 .A245
   ____ RC514 .A26
   ____ RC514 .A4213

   b)
   ____ E580 .W66
   ____ E580 .W7
   ____ E71 .W24

   c)
   ____ 810.2
   ____ 810.02
   ____ 810.122

Answers: 3a) 1, 2, 3; 3b) 2, 3, 1; 3c) 3, 1, 2

Four

Finding Periodicals

Maps show you the way; they guide you on your journey. You shouldn't go on a long road trip without a map, especially if you want to arrive at your destination on time or without getting lost. In the same way, you shouldn't begin your search for articles without first consulting a periodical index. The most efficient way to find articles is to use the periodical indexes usually found online via your library Web site. These indexes often contain tremendous amounts of information, providing records of the contents of numerous publications that sometimes span decades.

Periodical indexes are like road maps for finding your way through magazines, journals, and newspapers, helping you to determine which issues will contain articles on your topic. While wandering around the periodical room and browsing is obviously an ineffective way to find articles, so is using commercial Web search engines, unless you're lucky. Although some periodicals have their own Web sites that might provide selected articles for free from current issues and maybe even selected ones from older issues, to access the full 'archives' you usually have to be a subscriber. It's especially important to remember that students can often get articles through their libraries, meaning that you don't always have to pay to get the materials you need.

Maps aren't very helpful unless you know your destination. As emphasized in Chapter 1, the first step on the road of research is defining your topic. So before you begin searching indexes for articles, it's a good idea to choose your subject. It's okay to have a broad topic, but, as you proceed with your research, you will have to hone in on a specific idea to pursue.

TYPES OF PERIODICALS

The next thing you have to decide is what type of articles you need. Although all periodicals are published on an on-going basis (daily, weekly, monthly, quarterly), there are different varieties of periodicals: scholarly journals, trade journals, general magazines, newspapers, and so on. Before proceeding further, you need to understand the important differences between types of periodicals since they, along with your topic, will determine which indexes you search.

When your professors instruct you to find journal articles, they usually don't have *People*, *Time*, or *Cosmopolitan* in mind. Professors generally want their students to use scholarly or academic journals in their research. These are periodicals containing articles written by experts in particular fields of study, frequently individuals affiliated with academic institutions. The terms 'journal' and 'magazine' are often used synonymously but this is misleading. You also shouldn't assume a journal is a scholarly journal just because the word 'journal' is in the title of the publication (like *Ladies Home Journal*). Another type of journal is also useful to those doing business research—the trade journal. Trade journals, such as *Advertising Age* and *Brandweek*, are periodicals written for people working in a specific industry, and should not be confused with scholarly journals.

Scholarly journals tend to be very specialized in their subject focus and are research oriented, containing examples of primary literature sources. Primary sources are those in which scholars report the findings of their own research (as opposed to secondary sources, which report on someone else's activities). Another characteristic of academic journal articles is that they are often 'peer reviewed.' This means that before an article is accepted, it must be deemed worthy of publication by an anonymous group of the author's colleagues. Academic journal articles usually have bibliographies at the end citing all the sources referred to in the text. Bibliographies can be helpful, leading you to a variety of sources that may aid in your research.

If you were to look at the table of contents of an issue of the *Journal of Popular Culture*, you'd see articles like "Why I Hate Abercrombie & Fitch: Essays on Race and Sexuality" or "Producing Containment: The Rhetorical Construction of Difference in *Will & Grace*." If you were to pick up a copy of *People*, on the other hand, you might see articles such as "Life after 'American Idol'" or "Brad's Pitt Stops." While the difference in content reflected in these titles is pretty obvious, the physical difference is also apparent. Magazines tend to be glossy publications with eye-catching covers, while journals often look dull—but, just as you should not 'judge a book by its cover,' don't overlook a periodical simply because of its appearance. Magazines are general-interest publications that you would find on a newsstand or in a bookstore, and are intended for a general audience. Although they may be easier and more enjoyable to read because they don't go into as much technical depth as scholarly journals, they are usually not as valuable for your own research unless your research is focused on contemporary popular culture.

INDEXES: YOUR ROAD MAPS FOR FINDING ARTICLES

When you need to find information in a nonfiction book, you can usually refer to an index located in the back. Instead of browsing through the entire book looking for what you need,

Table 4.1: Journals vs. Magazines.	
JOURNAL ARTICLES	MAGAZINE ARTICLES
• Written for a specialized audience	• Written for a more general audience
• Articles by subject experts	• Articles by journalists and generalists
• Authors from academic institutions	• Authors are staff writers or freelancers
• Highly focused topics	• More generalized topics
• Primary research or literature reviews	• Secondary sources
• Peer-reviewed	• Edited but not peer-reviewed
• Include bibliographies	• No bibliographies
• (Most) have dull-looking covers	• Glossy covers and eye-catching graphics

you simply turn to the alphabetically arranged index and look up your subject to determine what page to turn to, saving a lot of time and effort. As an indication of how essential indexes are for finding information effectively, many Web sites are also beginning to provide 'site indexes' or 'site maps' which link you to the page you want within a site. Periodical indexes do the same sort of thing by referring you to articles in specific issues of various periodicals. There are many different indexes, each one focusing on periodicals in a particular subject area, and most of these indexes are now available in a computerized format.

Print Indexes

Let me tell you one of those 'walking ten miles through the snow to school' stories that will really make you appreciate the fact that you go to college in the 21st century. How did students find articles before there were online indexes? They laboriously leafed through volume after heavy volume of the print indexes that took up a lot of space on library shelves.

The most popular index used to be the *Readers' Guide to Periodical Literature,* with annual volumes, each indexing a year's worth of periodicals, going back to 1900. You'd look up your subject and sometimes find a cross-reference to another, often broader and less useful, heading elsewhere in the index (for example: **DISCO dancing. See Dance.**). Sometimes it was hard to find any articles on a complex topic if it could not adequately be defined by a single subject heading. You would have to skim through many irrelevant articles under a broad heading in order to find the specific one that you needed. There was no way to search a print index by keyword, only by subject heading, and we now know how difficult that can sometimes be. Electronic indexes are such a great improvement over their print equivalents that you should consider yourself lucky and never ever complain about having to do research.

Print indexes are actually still published but you will seldom need to use them. They can occasionally be useful when you need to find an article from an older issue of a periodical, perhaps dating from before 1980. Let's say, for example, you wanted to find some articles about the phenomenon of disco in the 1970s. You want articles written at that time, not ones written more recently. If your library does not subscribe to the electronic Readers' Guide Retrospective or another electronic index that covers periodicals from that time period, you will need to find the volumes of the print version of the *Readers' Guide*.

There are four *citations* or references under the heading

DISCO music

   Disco tech. A Kopkind. New Times 12:52 Ja 8 '79

   Does disco cause cancer? W. Anderson. il Stereo R
      41:8 Ag '78

   Heatwave rises from the valley of disco. A. Peck. il
      Roll Stone p. 25-6 Je 1 '78

   How to put together a party's worth of disco
      sound. S. Ditlea. Glamour 76:80 N '78

      See also

   Disco groups

   Discotheques

   Phonograph records—Disco music

   Radio broadcasting—Music

Figure 4.1: A sample listing in the print *Readers' Guide to Periodical Literature*.

of **DISCO music** in the volume from 1979; as will be explained later, these citations provide all the information you need to find the articles. Appearing under the citations are four *See also* references directing you to other listings of pertinent articles within the same volume, including the cross-reference **Phonograph records—Disco music** which sounds pretty ancient. It's interesting to see how subjects evolve. In the 1973 volume of *Readers' Guide*, there were no articles on disco, and in the next volume there was only one. But by 1978 disco was a big part of American culture, as indicated by the larger number of articles about disco music and discotheques.

Index Selection

Just as you don't usually rely on a world atlas when taking a road trip in a particular state, but instead use a road map of the specific area you're traveling in, you don't use *Readers' Guide* for every topic. Since many topics are interdisciplinary in nature, you can certainly find articles in more than one index. There is a wide variety of indexes focusing on particular fields of interest.

For example, if you were doing a paper about the future of space travel, you might want to consult a resource like *General Science Index.* To find articles about the growing interest in space tourism, you could take a look in a business index like InfoTrac Business ASAP. Biography Reference Bank would provide citations to material about famous astronauts. You could also use a newspaper index like the *New York Times Index* to find newspaper articles on this topic.

When selecting which index to use, first become familiar with the ones available at your library. How do you find out which print and online periodical indexes your library has? Click the link on the library homepage that will bring up the list of available resources. This link has no standard name. It could be called many things, including any of the following: 'Find Articles,' 'Databases,' 'Electronic Databases,' 'Research Tools,' or simply 'Resources.' The databases may be grouped by subject or type—such as indexes that provide full text, reference sources, online books, or journals—to aid in your selection. There is often an alphabetical listing too. If you don't know how to get to the indexes, ask a librarian.

Access to indexes and other resources on your library Web site is often restricted. The library pays a subscription fee for each database and signs a contract agreement to 'license' these databases. License agreements define who is allowed to use a particular database. Sometimes you can use them only within the library, or you may be able to get to them from the library's homepage in your dorm room or at any computer on campus. Another way of restricting access is to implement passwords (often your student ID number) so you can use the resources from virtually any location on or off campus. Some libraries also use proxy servers, allowing students to access restricted resources from off campus.

Consider the following when deciding which index to search:

- **What is the subject focus of the index?** Choose an index that pertains to the subject area for your topic. You don't have to limit yourself to one single index.
- **What type of material does it cover?** Does it cover scholarly journals, trade journals, general magazines, newspapers, or a mixture? Your decision to use or not use a particular index will depend on your needs.
- **What years are indexed?** Be aware of what general time period is covered by the index. Bear in mind, for example, that you wouldn't want to search an electronic index that only includes citations for journal articles published in the 1990s or later if what you really want are articles published in the 1960s.

What Does an Index Tell You?

Periodical indexes provide lists of citations for articles on the subject you search for, as displayed in Figure 4.1 (from a print index) and Figure 4.2 (from an electronic index). A citation is a reference to an article that provides all the information you need to locate that article. Print and electronic indexes provide the same basic information in their citations including the title of the article itself, the title of the periodical it appears in, the date and page numbers. The author's name is often included but is not essential.

Some citations also include volume and issue numbers, especially for academic journals. Instead of a particular date, a journal citation may just include a year. In this case, the volume and issue number are necessary. The volume number generally refers to the year of publication. Volume 23 would refer to the 23rd year the journal was published. If a journal is a quarterly, the issue numbers would go from 1 to 4; if it's a monthly 1 to 12.

1. MOVERS AND SHAKERS. (cover story) By: Sale, Anabel Unity. Community Care. 9/28/2006 Issue 1642, p32-33, 2p, 6c; (AN 22997583)
   Notes: This title is not held by UNH
   📖 HTML Full Text

2. _Disco_ Anthropology. By: Yuan, Jada. New York, 9/4/2006, Vol. 39 Issue 31, p24-24, 1p, 17bw; (AN 22289951)
   Notes: This title is held by UNH
   Find It ⊙UNH

3. From Russia, With Love and Ambivalence. By: Bleyer, Jennifer. New York Times, 4/24/2005, Vol. 154 Issue 53194, The City p12-12, 1/3p; (AN 16991342)
   Notes: This title is held by UNH
   Find It ⊙UNH

4. The Göteborg discotheque fire: posttraumatic stress, and school adjustment as reported by the primary victims 18 months later. By: Broberg, Anders G.; Dyregrov, Atle; Lilled, Lars. Journal of Child Psychology & Psychiatry, Apr2005, Vol. 46 Issue 4, p1279-1286, 8p, 3 charts; DOI: 10.1111/j.1469-7610.2005.01439.x; (AN 19519036)
   Cited References [32]
   Notes: This title is held by UNH
   📄 PDF Full Text (98K)

5. Queer for The Ear: Extreme Make Overs for _Disco_ Dance Classics (Music). Lesbian News, Jun2004, Vol. 29 Issue 11, p38-38, 1/8p, 1bw; (AN 13407846)
   Notes: This title is not held by UNH
   📖 HTML Full Text 📄 PDF Full Text (389K)

Figure 4.2: A list of citations from Academic Search.

Here is one of the citations from Figure 4.1 giving you all the information you need to find it:

Does disco cause cancer? W. Anderson. il Stereo R 41:8 Ag '78

- Does disco cause cancer? (article title)
- W. Anderson (author)
- il (illustrated)
- Stereo R (title of the publication, in this case *Stereo Review*; an alphabetical listing of periodical abbreviations appears in the front of each volume of the index)
- 41:8 Ag '78 (volume 41, page 8, August 1978)

Because of the space constraints of print indexes, citations are written in a shorthand that can sometimes be hard to decipher. Citations from electronic indexes are often easier to understand because they are not abbreviated to such a great extent. In addition to the basic information, online indexes often provide summaries of the articles, which can be a great aid in evaluating and selecting articles for your research.

Electronic indexes often eliminate the need to locate the article because they provide the text for many of the articles cited. If you see an article title that looks like it will be a helpful source, however, don't pass it by simply because only the citation is available. Instead, check to see if your library subscribes to the periodical cited. You don't have to limit yourself to the articles that are available online.

While Figure 4.1 was an entry from a print index, Figure 4.2 displays a list of recent citations on the subject of disco obtained via an electronic index called Academic Search. You can click on any of these titles to view the full citation. Later in this chapter, you will find out more about obtaining the full text and what HTML, PDF, and 'Find It' mean. To see an example of a complete record, see Figure 4.3, which describes an article on a different topic. You will notice that the information is spelled out a bit more clearly than

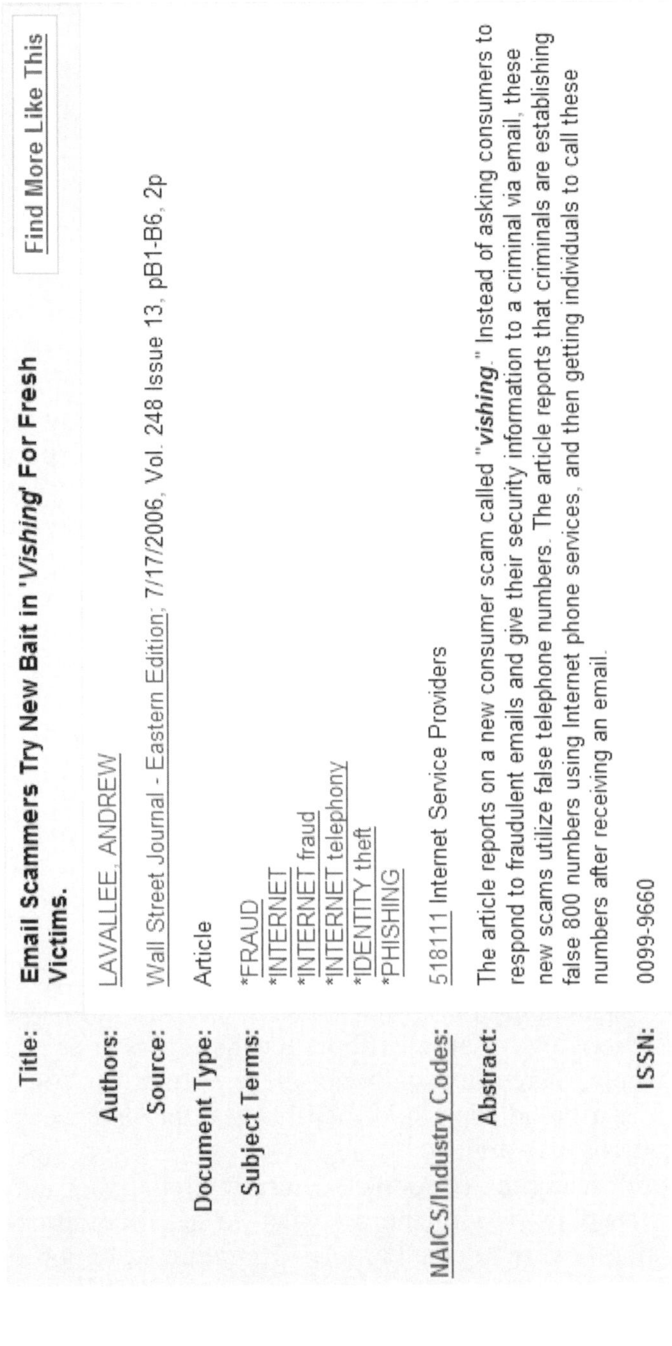

Title:	**Email Scammers Try New Bait in '*Vishing*' For Fresh Victims.**	Find More Like This

Authors:	LAVALLEE, ANDREW
Source:	Wall Street Journal - Eastern Edition; 7/17/2006; Vol. 248 Issue 13; pB1-B6; 2p
Document Type:	Article
Subject Terms:	*FRAUD *INTERNET *INTERNET fraud *INTERNET telephony *IDENTITY theft *PHISHING
NAICS/Industry Codes:	518111 Internet Service Providers
Abstract:	The article reports on a new consumer scam called "*vishing*." Instead of asking consumers to respond to fraudulent emails and give their security information to a criminal via email, these new scams utilize false telephone numbers. The article reports that criminals are establishing false 800 numbers using Internet phone services, and then getting individuals to call these numbers after receiving an email.
ISSN:	0099-9660

Figure 4.3: Full record for an article in Academic Search.

in the print *Readers' Guide* because space is less restricted in online environments. Abstracts can also be quite lengthy, offering far more information than is available in print indexes, where summaries are generally briefer if they are included at all.

SEARCHING INDEXES

Subject vs. Keyword Searching

As explained in Chapter 2, there are no universally standardized subject headings used to classify articles the way there are in the Library of Congress subject headings for books, though each database does have its own methodology. Many databases provide a 'thesaurus' or 'subject list,' which can be helpful for finding the right heading. If you look up **adolescents** in EBSCOhost's 'subject terms,' for example, you will be instructed to use **teenagers** instead, since this is the official heading. Using a database's thesaurus is like looking up Library of Congress headings in the 'red books.'

A good example of the inconsistency of subject headings is provided by the cover story from the August 1999 *U.S. News & World Report,* entitled "Schools Turn Off the Tap," which concerns steps being taken by colleges to curtail binge drinking. Notice the difference between the headings given to the same exact article in two different databases in Table 4.2.

Because of these inconsistencies, you should start with keyword searching unless your topic is very straightforward. If you're looking for articles about a certain person or place, for example, there are usually not many variations. You can also enter a broad topic and then browse through the subheadings for that subject.

As with searching for books, determining the appropriate subject headings is still the best way to get a comprehensive listing of very relevant articles. Keyword searching pre-

Table 4.2: Example of Inconsistency in Subject Headings.

In EBSCOhost Academic Search:	In InfoTrac Expanded Academic ASAP:
• drinking of alcoholic beverages—universities and colleges	• alcohol—usage
• universities and colleges—social life and customs	• fraternal organizations—social aspects
• college students—alcohol use	• universities and colleges—alcohol use

sents the problems of finding irrelevant material or not finding all the relevant material. But even if you find just one really good article through keyword searching, you can take a look at the subject headings given the article and backtrack, clicking on an appropriate heading. For example, if your topic is about how identity thieves are using the Internet to steal personal information you might enter a keyword search for **identity theft and internet** in EBSCOhost's Academic Search. The record for the first citation is displayed in Figure 4.3.

Maybe you had no idea what 'vishing' was but now you do if you read the abstract. Notice the subject headings for this article. **Phishing** sounds a lot like 'vishing' so you click on this heading to retrieve all the articles on this subject. By doing this, you come up with a set of articles concerned with a method of identity theft that you knew nothing about. **Internet fraud** is another heading that you might want to explore further also. So always look at the headings of appropriate articles. They could lead you to a gold mine of related information.

Broadening Your Search by Searching the Full Text

If you haven't found many articles and need more information, you can broaden your search in many databases by searching the complete text of available articles. Most databases automatically limit their searches to the citation and abstract. On the opening search screen for EBSCOhost, you can click on the option 'search within full text articles' while in InfoTrac's keyword search mode, the default is searching 'in title, citation, abstract,' but you can change this to 'in entire article content.' Be forewarned, however, that full-text searching increases your chances of finding irrelevant material much more so than when only the abstract is searched. One of your search terms may only be mentioned in passing and have very little to do with the main focus of the article. An article about fraternities, for example, might mention binge drinking, while the article is really about the history of fraternities.

Narrowing Your Search

Limiters

You can also limit your search in very specific ways if you have found too much. The following limiters are commonly available in many databases:

- Limiting by Periodical—Most databases allow you to search a single periodical, so if you have a specific journal in mind, you can narrow your search in this way. Before doing this, find out if the database does, indeed, index the source you are interested in. You can usually find a list of the sources covered online. In EBSCOhost, for example, there is a 'Publications' button to click on the top of the page.
- Limiting by Date—There is often the option of searching only a certain date or range of dates.

- Limiting to Articles with Full Text—In databases that contain the complete text for only selected articles, you can limit your results by searching for only the citations that also have the text. Even though this makes things easier for you, however, just be aware that you might be missing some wonderful sources.
- Limiting to Peer-Reviewed Journals—One final limiter in a number of databases that index academic journals, including Expanded Academic ASAP and Academic Search, is limiting to "peer-reviewed" publications. This method will only find articles in scholarly journals that are refereed, meaning that an article must be accepted for publication by a group of scholars.

Figure 4.4 displays the 'Refine Search' form in Academic Search, which includes ways to limit your search as well as ways to expand it.

Proximity Operators

In addition to Boolean connectors, you may be able to use something called a proximity operator in certain databases. This method allows you to narrow your search by specifying that two or more words appear within a certain number of words of each other. Proximity operators are usually composed of the letter N for 'near' or W for 'within' and then a number to specify the number of words. You place the proximity operator between the words that are to be searched. For example, **Television N5 violence** in EBSCOhost will find 'television violence' as well as 'violence in movies and television.' **Television w/5 violence** in LexisNexis™ will do the same thing. Infotrac Expanded Academic ASAP includes an automatic one-word proximity operator when you enter more than one word in a single search box. That is, instead of placing an invisible Boolean AND operator between the words it tries to identify articles that include your search terms in direct proximity to one another. The words do not

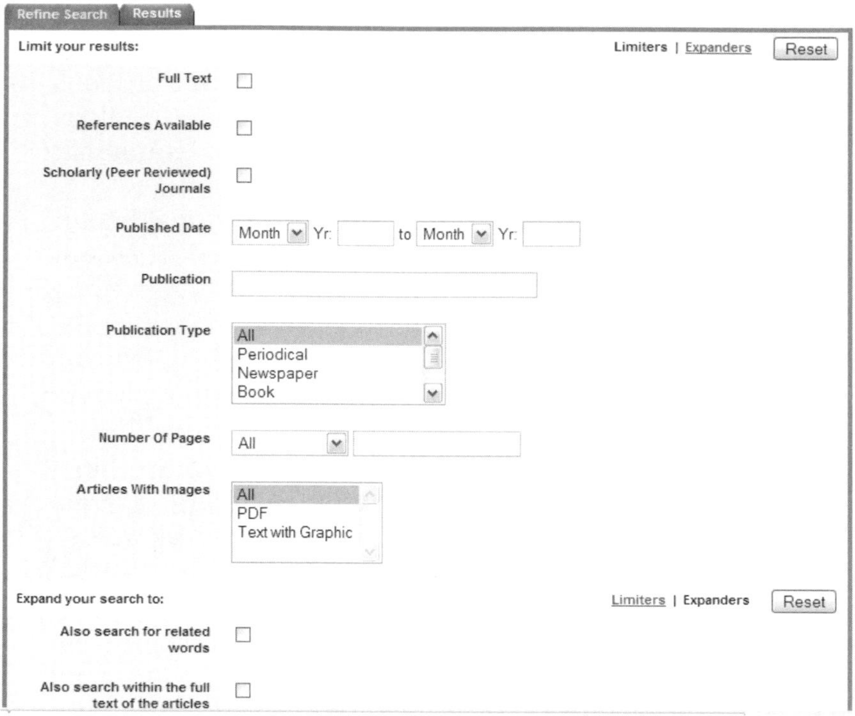

Figure 4.4: "Refine Search" form in Academic Search.

have to appear in the order in which you typed them, but they can have no more than one word between them. Depending on what database you are in, however, word order may be important. For instance, the word **television** might have to be before **violence** in the example above. So once again, consult those help files to find out.

Field-Specific Searching

Generally, when you do a basic keyword search, the entire citation as well as the abstract for each record in the database are searched automatically, even though the chances of retrieving irrelevant articles are increased if the abstracts are searched. Limiting your search to certain fields, as discussed in Chapter 2, can be very effective in focusing your search and reducing the number of irrelevant articles you find.

When you go to the advanced searching screen in Academic Search, as displayed in Figure 4.5, you will see a form that includes several pull-down menus. The menu lets you choose which fields to search. You can choose nothing which will do a 'default fields' search for your term in the citations and abstracts, or 'TX All Text' which will find those records which contain your term anywhere in the article, or 'TI Title' which searches only the article titles, narrowing your search substantially. Other fields include: 'SU Subject Terms,' 'AB Abstract,' and 'SO Journal Name.'

You can combine up to three field-specific searches in this database to really hone in on your subject. The more boxes you fill in on this form, the narrower your search will be.

Fields that can be searched differ in just about every database depending on what would be useful to the searcher. In the General News database in LexisNexis™ Academic as displayed in Figure 4.6, the 'Guided News' search form lets you search for words in the headline, the lead paragraph, the complete text, the caption, and the author. When using this database, be sure to check the date range that the search will cover, as it defaults to 'Previous six months' despite the fact that the range of available choices is quite large.

GETTING YOUR HANDS ON THE ARTICLES

So once you know where to go, how do you actually get there? In other words, once you have citations, how do you get your hands on the articles? If you've used an electronic index, you may be able to retrieve the full text online. Still, electronic indexes provide many citations without the text. Don't pass these by just because you have to do some extra work. If you've used a print index, you'll definitely have to track down the articles. Since every library is arranged a bit

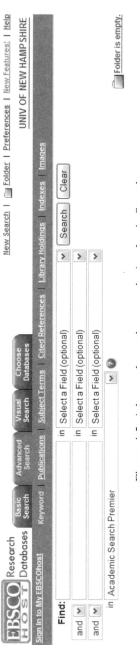

Figure 4.5: Advanced search screen in Academic Search.

LexisNexis   · Home | Sources | Site Map | What's New | Help

Quick News Search | **Guided News Search**   Tips

Academic Search Forms

> Quick Info
> News
> Business
> Legal Research
> Medical
> Reference

Search for Other Information

> Congressional
> Statistical

Step One: Select a news category -- *Entry Required*

Select a News Category

Step Two: Select a news source -- *Entry Required*

All Available Documents   Source List

Step Three: Enter search terms -- *Entry Required*

		in	Headline, Lead Paragraph(s), Terms
and		in	Headline, Lead Paragraph(s), Terms
and		in	Headline, Lead Paragraph(s), Terms

Step Four: Narrow to a specific date range -- *Optional*

⦿ Previous six months

○ From: To:

Step Five: Search this publication title(s) -- *Optional*

Search   Clear Form

Terms and Conditions | Privacy

Copyright © 2006 LexisNexis, a division of Reed Elsevier Inc. All Rights Reserved.

Figure 4.6: "Guided News" search form in LexisNexis™ Academic.

differently, the paths will be somewhat varied, but I'll give you a general idea of how to arrive at your destination in the sometimes confusing land of periodicals.

Formats

You will find articles in three basic formats: hard copy, microfilm or microfiche, and electronic. While hard copies are the actual physical magazines, newspapers, or journals, microfilm provides a space-saving copy on film that can be read and reproduced by using a microfilm machine. Believe it or not, at one time, microfilm was considered the latest in information technology, since a whole month's worth of newspapers or a year's worth of periodical issues could fit on one roll of film. Today, microfilm seems outdated, awkward, and simply a pain to use. Still, it is common in many libraries and will be around for some time to come. Microfiche is a type of microfilm in sheet format which holds many pages.

The electronic format available through online indexes is either full text or full image. In Academic Search Premier (displayed in Figure 4.2), for example, these options are referred to as 'HTML Full Text,' meaning that a Web page containing the text of the article will appear if you click on that link, or 'PDF Full Text.' PDF stands for 'Portable Document Format,' meaning that if you select that option, an exact replica of the article will appear. Acrobat Reader or a similar program is required to open PDF files, but as it is freely available online, this requirement should not present a difficulty. Expanded Academic ASAP includes some articles in a hybrid format whereby the articles are in HTML, but with images embedded. In most databases, files can be printed, e-mailed, or downloaded regardless of the format.

A growing number of libraries now subscribe to individual journals in electronic format. Through such services as JSTOR, Project Muse, and EBSCOhost's Electronic Journal Service (EJS), articles can often be obtained in PDF. Many libraries that subscribe to e-journals include a record for these titles in their online catalog, so that if you look up the journal title, you will be provided with a Web link rather than a call number. Just click and let your fingers do the walking.

Suppose you have searched a database such as EBSCOhost and found a citation that has neither the full text nor full image. In some libraries, you will see the 'Find It' icon like the one seen in second citation in Figure 4.2. If you click on this link, you will be directed either to another database available through your library Web site which will provide the article, or to the record for the appropriate journal in your library's online catalog. This is called SFX linking and can save you further time and frustration.

Generally, full-text electronic sources are recent in their focus. Readers' Guide Retrospective, which provides coverage all the way back to 1890s, is an exception, as are a growing number of databases that have an historical focus. Accessible Archives provides access to the full text of numerous publications from the 18th and 19th centuries through such databases as The Civil War: A Newspaper Perspective, Godey's Lady's Book, and American County Histories to 1900. ProQuest Historical Newspapers is a database that provides the digitized full images of every page of the *New York Times* and the *Wall Street Journal* back to their beginnings in the 19th century. Other newspapers available through this database include the *Washington Post* and the *Christian Science Monitor*. Keep in mind that for many topics, the latest information may not be the greatest, so these resources will be useful.

You may be tempted to use only those articles that are readily available online so that you can avoid using microform or having to track down the hard copy in the periodical room. By disregarding any index citations that might send you to the microform or periodical room, however, you may miss out on the most helpful information for your paper. You should not pick a periodical source based on its format, but rather on its content. In the end, you'll be better off because having better sources makes it easier to write your research paper.

Periodical Organization

While the nonelectronic copies of older magazines and newspapers are generally stored on microform, past issues of scholarly journals are often in book form, a year's worth of issues bound into a single volume. Not all libraries organize their periodicals in the same way. In some libraries, periodicals (both hard copy and microform) are arranged alphabetically by title. In other libraries, each periodical is assigned a call number depending on its subject focus. The same rules of Library of Congress or Dewey Decimal call numbers apply. Bound volumes of journals arranged by call number may be shelved in the periodical room or in the same stacks where circulating books are found. Your library may even have closed stacks so that you must request the material and don't have to worry about how it is arranged. Familiarize yourself with the method of organization used to arrange periodicals in your library. Don't hesitate to ask a librarian for help if you can't easily determine the organizational scheme yourself.

What If Your Library Doesn't Have It?

Tens of thousands of magazines and journals are published in the world today, along with thousands of newspapers. With so many periodicals available, a single library can't subscribe to every one, so academic libraries generally subscribe to what are known as the core (or most important) journals in those fields in which the college specializes. They may also get some of the peripheral (or less essential) journals in these same fields, as well as many general magazines, major newspapers like the *New York Times*, and the local papers for the area in which the library is located.

You can usually search for a periodical title in the same way you look for a book title in the online catalog. If your library doesn't subscribe to the periodical you need to complete your paper or doesn't have it available in electronic format, don't lose hope. If you have allotted yourself sufficient time for obstacles along the way, you can take advantage of the resources of other libraries.

Your library Web site may provide links to the other libraries in your area, and you can determine if another library has a particular periodical by searching its online catalog. If your library is part of a consortium, there may be an electronic list of periodicals so you can search many libraries at once. When you have determined the location of the periodical you need, you can either go to the library yourself to copy the article or have a copy sent to your own library, if such a delivery service is available. Sometimes requests for articles can even be submitted through your library Web site.

If the periodical cannot be located in the immediate vicinity, your library can obtain it through interlibrary loan (ILL). Even if the article you need is in an obscure scholarly journal held by only a handful of libraries in the country, your library's ILL department can request this article and usually get it to you within a week or two. The time factor involved here is the main drawback of ILL and the reason that many students, starting their papers too late, cannot take advantage of this valuable free service. Remember, though, that ILL is a free service, so you should not hesitate to take advantage of it.

Finding articles is an essential part of your research. For some narrow or very recent topics, articles may provide you with the only information you can find. So don't get lost and frustrated. Keep going in the right direction by using the appropriate periodical indexes.

Evaluating Your Sources: The PACAC Method—Content

DOES THIS SOURCE ADEQUATELY ADDRESS MY TOPIC? Perhaps the most fundamental question you should ask when evaluating a source is whether it adequately provides you with the information you need. Does it answer the main questions that you have about your topic? The records you find using indexes, online catalogs, and periodical indexes, and the results you get from search engines do not always have enough information to evaluate the material described. Even when you are given an abstract in an article citation or a table of contents in an online book record, you may not get a clear idea of what the source will really provide.

An effective way to thoroughly evaluate content is to skim through the actual book, article, or Web site to see how extensively your topic is addressed. For a book, you might also look up your topic in the book's index to get a sense of how many pages are devoted to it. Even though the source may have sounded great initially, you may realize that it won't really help you. Although you may decide not to use a source and it may feel like you have wasted your time, this is certainly not the case because you increase your knowledge throughout the evaluation process.

EXERCISES

1) Judging from the title alone, identify each of the following periodicals as a popular magazine (M) or a scholarly journal (J):

   a) ___ *Child Development*
   b) ___ *U.S. News and World Report*
   c) ___ *Yankee*
   d) ___ *Sex Roles*
   e) ___ *Public Relations Review*
   f) ___ *The New Yorker*
   g) ___ *Saturday Evening Post*
   h) ___ *Popular Mechanics*
   i) ___ *Studies in Latin American Popular Culture*
   j) ___ *Journal of Popular Film and Television*

2) A search for articles can usually be limited by all of the following except:

   a) publication date
   b) academic affiliation of author
   c) full text availability
   d) type of publication

3) Which of the following searches using proximity operators would locate more records:

   a) Mars W5 water
   b) Mars N5 water
   c) Mars N8 water
   d) Mars W8 water

Answers: 1a) J, 1b) M, 1c) M, 1d) J, 1e) J, 1f) M, 1g) M, 1h) M, 1i) J, 1j) J; 2) b; 3) c.

Five

Exploring Reference Sources

Imagine you have gotten lost while driving through a desert. It's the hottest time of the day, and the road ahead of you stretches on for miles; you're not even sure if you're going in the right direction or if you should have gone the other way at that last fork in the road. You're running low on fuel, you can't find a map in the car, and, to top it off, you're thirsty and have no more water! It's been 50 miles since you passed a gas station and you have no idea how long it will be before you come to another.

This unfortunate situation can be compared to the dreaded 'library scavenger hunt' that requires students to answer a series of trivial questions using reference sources. The intention is positive—to have students learn how to use the library's resources, especially those in the reference room or their computerized versions online. But the result is often negative—a frustrated student who can't wait to leave the library or the library's Web site. You shouldn't be sent to the library to complete such an assignment or any research project without some clear directions.

Reference sources enable you to find quick answers to your questions as well as broad information on paper topics, either to get you started with your research or to check a fact before handing in your final draft. They are the basic necessities of research, just as water and fuel are indispensable when driving through the desert. This chapter will introduce you to the major categories of reference sources by posing some questions that might remind you of the board game "Trivial Pursuit." The answers will be provided to satisfy your curiosity, but more important, I will explain how to find the answers effectively. If you encounter a similar sort of question in the future, you'll know where to go. This chapter will highlight the types of sources that are considered among the most helpful for reference and will give you a few examples. No college library will have every source mentioned in this chapter, but a good library will have a large percentage of them, as well as many other titles that fall into the general categories of reference material discussed. As you will discover, taking advantage of these resources will ultimately be far more reliable and far more rewarding than a quick search of a collaborative online encyclopedia like Wikipedia.

Because so many sources that you previously had to use in the library are now available online, a virtual 'Reference Room' is emerging on many library Web sites. But don't forget about the physical reference room. There are still many reference sources that are only available in print, and sometimes it's simply easier to open up an encyclopedia to an article on your subject. Like Wikipedia, reference rooms bring together a tremendous amount of information in one place, making it easy to find what you are searching for.

ENCYCLOPEDIAS: A GOOD STARTING POINT

Q: How much did the *Titanic* weigh?

A: The *Titanic* weighed 46,328 tons, or over 92 million pounds! (I still don't understand how such a heavy thing could float, but that's a research question for another day.) Source: *Encyclopedia Americana,* International ed., 2005, vol. 26, 785.

Encyclopedias, whether computerized or in their traditional place on the bookshelves, are often a good place to start your research because they provide concise, factual overviews on a vast number of subjects. Encyclopedias are probably one of the first things that come to mind when you hear the term 'reference books.' Among other things, encyclopedia articles can help you identify keywords and concepts related to your research topic. They are thus a great way to scout out the territory before you plunge into more sophisticated or in-depth resources.

You will usually find the volumes of general encyclopedias in the A call number section of the reference room if your library uses the LC Classification or in the 030s if Dewey is used, along with other general works.

The most scholarly and in-depth encyclopedia is the *Encyclopaedia Britannica*. Here are others you are likely to find:

- *Encyclopedia Americana*—This work is suitable for college-level research.
- *Academic American Encyclopedia*—This source is also a good starting point for your research projects.
- *Collier's Encyclopedia*—Written on a high school level, this encyclopedia is intended for a more general audience.
- *World Book Encyclopedia*—This work should be a last resort because it is not intended for college-level research.

Many encyclopedias are now available online. Using the Web version of the *Encyclopaedia Britannica* (www. britannica.com), you can read the first paragraph of the *Titanic* entry—after a barrage of pop-up ads—but the full text will not be available to you unless you are a paying subscriber or a student at a school that subscribes. There is also Microsoft's Encarta Online encyclopedia which has no print equivalent (http://encarta.msn.com/encnet/refpages/ artcenter.aspx). Using Encarta, you can find the weight of the *Titanic*, as well as information on thousands of other common topics, but you also have to look at an annoying amount of advertising.

We'll be discussing the evaluation of Web sites later on, but a few words are appropriate here. If something is available for free, it's usually of a lower quality or includes a lot of advertising. For example, online encyclopedias like Britannica and Encarta allow you to access some information for free, but only after you have had to view a number of advertisements, and they often do not provide complete entries unless you are a paying subscriber. Libraries must subscribe to most of the good computerized resources I will discuss just as you subscribe to cable TV to get most commercial-free programming. If your library's Web site provides links to Web-based reference sources, these sources have probably been selected because of their quality. So be a bit cautious when using the Web for reference sources. And be extremely skeptical if you feel the urge to simply use a Web search engine to find the answer to your question—you will probably retrieve a lot of irrelevant junk and even inaccurate information (but more about that later).

The Importance of Consulting the Index

Q: Who were the Plastic People of the Universe?
A: No, they weren't Saturday morning TV cartoon characters. This was the name of a Czechoslovakian band whose members were arrested in the mid-1970s, along with other intellectuals, artists, and students who belonged to the Charter 77 movement for Czech independence, which protested the repressive measures imposed after the Soviet invasion. The band's arrest motivated the playwright Vaclav Havel and others to sign a manifesto demanding respect for human and civil rights.
    Source: *Encyclopedia Americana*, International ed., 2005, vol. 8, 411.

Often, the most important part of an encyclopedia or any reference source or book is its index. Without it you may never find what you need. If you look up 'Plastic People of the Universe' alphabetically in the P volume of the *Encyclo-*

pedia Americana, for example, you won't find it. If your subject is not listed alphabetically in an encyclopedia, it's probably not broad enough to have its own entry. Look it up in the index, which is the last volume of the set. If you look up 'Plastic People of the Universe' in the index, you are directed to the broader heading of 'Czechoslovakia.'

The index is also handy because you can locate all the entries relating to your topic. For instance, if you look up 'deserts' in the index volume of *Encyclopedia Americana*, you'll be referred to a number of subtopics in addition to 'dust devils.' These topics, often in different volumes, all relate to the main topic, such as specific places (Death Valley and the Mojave Desert) and related topics (cactus and oasis). The index leads you to more information than would be contained in the D volume alone. It's similar to the online catalog providing you with cross references for books.

Indexes are the key to using most reference sources, and are also helpful in finding information in many nonfiction books in the circulating collection. If you're having trouble finding the information that you need in a particular source, look for an alphabetical index, either in the back of a one-volume source or in the final volume of a multivolume set (like a general encyclopedia).

Many electronic reference sources also utilize a computerized version of a back-of-book index. These are not indexes in the traditional sense. You might think that since databases are searchable by keywords that an index would be unnecessary, but users are starting to realize that they can wander just as aimlessly through a Web site as through a book, so site designers are incorporating indexes into their products to serve the same purpose. Instead of looking up your subject and turning to a certain page in a book, however, you click on your subject and go to a particular page within a site. The FirstGov.gov Web site, which offers access to a wide variety of U.S. government documents and resources, has a useful site index, partially displayed in Figure 5.1.

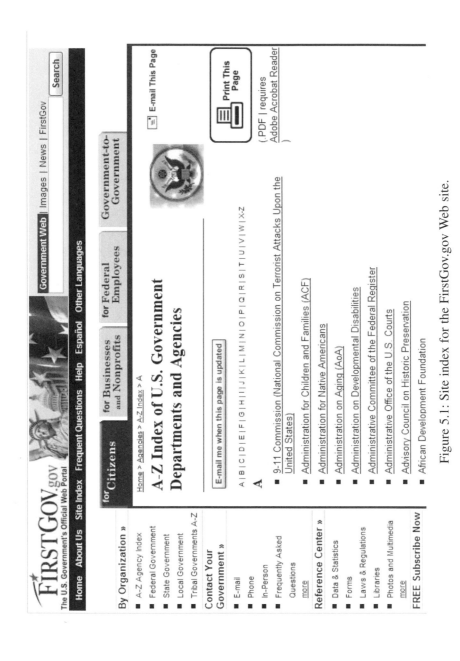

Figure 5.1: Site index for the FirstGov.gov Web site.

Subject-Specific Encyclopedias: Off the Main Drag

Q: How did the mood ring, that short-lived jewelry fad of the 1970s, really work? And why did Sophia Loren's mood ring make tabloid headlines in 1975?
A: Inside the stone of the mood ring were heat-sensitive liquid crystals derived through a chemical process from sheep's wool, the same stuff that had been used for years in hospital thermometers. In 1975 Sophia Loren, an Academy Award–winning Italian actress, stopped a press conference because to her horror her mood ring had turned black—a very bad omen, indeed!
Source: Jane and Michael Stern, *The Encyclopedia of Bad Taste* (New York: HarperCollins, 1990), 218.

You won't find any entries for mood rings in traditional general encyclopedias. This is where subject-specific encyclopedias sometimes come in handy. The subjects covered by the *Encyclopedia of Bad Taste* include a variety of fads of the 1970s, such as mood rings, disco, and bell bottoms (which experienced a revival a few years ago), as well as the short-lived phenomena of other decades.

Whereas each major general encyclopedia consists of many volumes, specialized encyclopedias are often just one volume, although some are multivolume sets. Besides including topics that may not be covered in general encyclopedias, these specialized books can go into much greater depth. More common specialized encyclopedias include the *Encyclopedia of Philosophy*, the *Encyclopedia of Religion*, and the *Encyclopedia of Popular Music*. Think of any major subject area and there's probably an encyclopedia that focuses on it.

There are also encyclopedias that focus on narrower subjects. In addition to the *Encyclopedia of Bad Taste* cited above, you might find such offbeat titles as the *Star Trek Encyclopedia* and the *Encyclopedia of Unbelief*. How do you locate these helpful sources? Keyword searching. For example, if you want to find out if there is an encyclopedia about sleep in your library, enter the keyword search **ency-clopedias and sleep** in the online catalog. This approach works well when you are looking for any subject-specific reference source. If you need a timeline of women's issues, try a search for **chronologies and women**; if you need a film term defined, search for **dictionaries and motion pictures**.

Sometimes encyclopedias have misleading titles that use the word 'dictionary' instead of 'encyclopedia.' For example, the *Dictionary of American History* is a multivolume work that contains long, detailed essays. Ordinarily, the basic difference between an encyclopedia and a dictionary is in the length of the entries: a dictionary implies brief definitions, while an encyclopedia contains lengthier entries. The line between these two types of sources sometimes gets a little blurry.

DICTIONARIES: WHAT DO YOU MEAN?

Q: What are the following: 1) phrenology, 2) puff-balls, 3) the best boy?
A:

1) Phrenology is the study of bumps on the head to determine personality traits.
2) Puff-balls are round stalkless mushrooms that discharge their spores in a cloud when touched.
3) If you've ever sat through the closing credits of a movie, you've probably wondered what the best boy does. Basically, he or she is the chief assistant to the chief electrician (or gaffer) on a motion picture set.

Sources:

1) *APA Dictionary of Psychology,* 2007, 700.
2) *Dictionary of American Regional English,* 2002, vol. 4, 365.
3) Ralph Singleton. *Filmmaker's Dictionary* (Hollywood, Calif.: Lone Eagle Publishing, 2000), 32.

Aside from the usual language dictionaries you consult from time to time, like *American Heritage* or *Webster's*, there are numerous specialized dictionaries such as those used above. As mentioned before, it's sometimes hard to draw the line between encyclopedias and dictionaries, but you could also consider these sources to be miniencyclopedias, providing brief definitions of terms used in a particular field of study in an alphabetical format.

There are many dictionaries available via the Web. Many are listed at the Ramapo Catskill Library System's site Best Online Reference Sites (http://ansernet.rcls.org/deskref/), a useful site that provides links to a wide variety of free, but surprisingly useful, online reference sources from encyclopedias and dictionaries to shoe-size conversion charts and used-car price guides.

ATLASES: BEYOND WHERE

Q: What were the five largest American cities in 1790? in 1870?
A: Philadelphia was actually the largest city in 1790, followed by New York and then Boston, Charleston, and Baltimore, all on the east coast. New York had overtaken Philadelphia by 1870. Brooklyn, which is today considered part of New York City (still the largest city), was third, followed by the more westerly cities of St. Louis and Chicago, indicating that the population of the country was shifting.
Source: Kenneth T. Jackson, ed., *Atlas of American History* (New York: Scribner's, 1984), 97, 177.

Atlases are commonly used to find out where a place is, how to get to it, what its geographic features are, and so on. They are handy for many research purposes, and most students are familiar with the straightforward atlases that are basically books containing maps of physical places. But atlases come in other varieties also. The question above reveals the usefulness of atlases that provide historical information, including population shifts over time. There are also atlases that focus on certain themes, such as the *Atlas of the Supernatural*. Although the maps in specialized atlases are usually supplemented with more text than in a general atlas, at the heart of these books are the maps that relate geography to a particular subject.

STATISTICAL SOURCES: HOW MUCH? HOW MANY?

Q: How many pounds of mozzarella cheese did the average American consume in 2002? Was this an increase over previous years?

A: In 2002 the average American ate 9.7 pounds of mozzarella. This was a substantial increase; in 1990, the amount was 6.9 pounds, and in 1980, only three pounds. Are we eating more pizza, perhaps? The answer was not in this source, but I'm sure this fact is somewhere.

Source: "Per Capita Consumption of Major Food Commodities," *Statistical Abstract of the United States* (Washington, D.C.: U.S. Government Printing Office, 2006), <www.census.gov/compendia/statab/health_nutrition/health.pdf> (26 July 2006).

Statistical Abstract of the United States, available both in print and online (www.census.gov/compendia/statab/), is a good place to check for any sort of national statistical information. It is an annual collection of statistics derived from the government census as well as from private sources. When you locate the appropriate table, be sure to note the year of the information given. Just because you're using the most recent volume doesn't mean you're getting current information. Sometimes the material might not be up to date because even online it takes time to collect, organize, and publish statistics. Note also, that the .gov suffix on this Web site indicates that it is a free U.S. government site. This marks it as a valuable resource, though you should remember that governments, like private individuals and organizations, have points of view, making it important to think critically about any information you find here.

Q: What percentage of U.S. households have three or more televisions? What percentage of people in Angola have one TV?

A: Of all U.S. households, 46 percent have three or more TVs. In Angola, at the other extreme, there are only 15 TVs for every 1,000 people—a rate of 1.5 percent. That means that if everyone in Angola wanted to watch TV at the same time, more than 66 people would have to gather around each set.

Source: *World Almanac and Book of Facts* (Mahwah, N.J.: Funk and Wagnalls, 2006), 278, 752.

If you require statistics for another country, a good place to check is the *World Almanac and Book of Facts*. Although this source includes primarily U.S. information, there is a long section that contains a brief entry for each country.

Other helpful sources for more in-depth international information:

- *Statesman's Yearbook*
- *Country Studies* (http://lcweb2.loc.gov/frd/cs)
- *CIA World Fact Book* (www.cia.gov/cia/publications/factbook/index.html).

The U.S. government is an excellent provider of statistical information and most of that information is now available online. In addition to *Statistical Abstract* and the sources listed above you can find a wide range of reliable sources at the FedStats Web site (www.fedstats.gov). FedStats provides links to the statistical information of over 100 federal agencies, including the Census Bureau, the CIA, NASA, the National Center for Education Statistics.

Government sources are also good because they are free. There are not too many Web site addresses in this book because many of the reliable reference sources are fee-based and your library may not subscribe. But government sources are available to anyone with Web access.

CHRONOLOGICAL SOURCES: WHEN?

Q: Who was the world's first 'space tourist?' When, where, and how did he go into space, and what did he pay for the trip?

A: On April 28, 2001, Dennis Tito, age 60, took off on a Russian Soyuz capsule with two cosmonauts to visit the International Space Station. The American businessman and former aerospace engineer paid 20 million dollars to the Russian space agency. The capsule docked with the space station on April 30 and Tito returned to Earth on May 6.

Source: "Space: First Tourist Visits Station," *Facts On File World News Digest,* 10 May 2001, <www.2facts.com> (June 29, 2006).

Facts On File World News Digest is a news service that provides biweekly summaries of world events. It's an excellent source for not only finding out when something happened but also who did it and other key information. In the print version, the digests are collected in a binder throughout the year and then bound into annual volumes. Your library might also subscribe to *Facts On File* on the Web.

Q: In what years did the following motion picture 'firsts' occur:
  1) sound movie, 2) Academy Awards, 3) drive-in theater, 4) psycho-slasher film?

A: 1) 1927 (*The Jazz Singer* with Al Jolson)
  2) 1929 (not a very suspenseful event since all the winners were announced in advance)
  3) 1933 (in New Jersey)
  4) 1978 (*Halloween*)

Source: Bruce Wetterau, *New York Public Library Book of Chronologies* (New York: Prentice Hall, 1990), 552–557.

For events of a more historic or thematic nature spanning a number of years, such as motion picture history, chronological reference sources are very helpful. Numerous books cover different historical topics or such themes as American wars (*Chronology of World War II*) or women's history (*Chronology of Women's History*). Try the keyword search method in the online catalog to find these sources (for example, **chronology and world war ii** or **timeline and world war ii**). There is also an excellent book called *Timetables of History* that, for any given year, will indicate what was going on simultaneously in such areas as politics, art, and society.

BIOGRAPHICAL SOURCES: WHO ARE YOU?

Q: What occupations did Martha Stewart pursue before gaining fame and fortune as a domestic maven and then infamy as a prison inmate?
A: Martha was employed as a professional caterer, a model, and a stockbroker. What a multitalented dynamo!

Source: "Martha Kostyra Stewart," *Marquis Who's Who*, 2006. Reproduced in *Biography Resource Center* (Farmington Hills, Mich.: Thomson Gale, 2006) <http://galenet.galegroup.com/servlet/BioRC>.

I used the online version of *Who's Who*, available from Biography Resource Center produced by InfoTrac. It includes such Who's Who sources as *Who Was Who in America* (for famous deceased people), *Who's Who in Entertainment*, and *Who's Who of American Women*, which are also available in print. These sources provide brief entries on notable people. There is usually contact information of some sort (not in the *Who Was Who* books, obviously), and all the important dates and accomplishments in the person's life.

Biography Resource Center also provides entries from a wide variety of other useful biographical reference sources, including the following titles which may likely be available in print at your library if you cannot access the online versions:

- *Concise Dictionary of American Literary Biography* and *Concise Dictionary of British Literary Biography*
- *Contemporary Authors*

- *Dictionary of American Biography*
- *Encyclopedia of World Biography*
- *Scribner Encyclopedia of American Lives*

Q: What profession did Secretary of State Condoleezza Rice plan to pursue when she began her studies at the University of Denver?

A: She wanted to be a concert pianist and intended to study music until she decided "that she lacked the talent to make it to the top of the highly competitive world of classical music."

Source: *Current Biography Yearbook* (New York: H. W. Wilson, 2001), 444–448.

If you want more in-depth information on a notable person, one place to turn is *Current Biography*. This series provides biographical essays on people who made an impact on the world in a particular year in some field—perhaps politics, sports, or entertainment. It is available both online and in print.

DIRECTORIES: GETTING IN TOUCH

Q: How can I contact the World Clown Association?

A: Call 800–336–7922 or e-mail *patlaywils@aol.com*. The organization, which "encourages the spread of the art of clowning around the world," has a Web site at http://www.worldclownassociation.com. You never knew those clowns were so organized, did you?

Source: *Encyclopedia of Associations*, 43rd ed. (Detroit: Gale Research, 2006), vol. 2, 2405.

Real people are great sources of information. Let's say you're doing a research paper on clowns and you want to interview someone to add a bit more depth to your paper. Or maybe you just want to be sent some literature in the mail on a particular organization or find out the address of its Web site. To identify organizations, learn their missions, and find out how to get in touch with them, use the *Encyclopedia of Associations* either online or in print. This is not an encyclopedia in the true sense; it is more accurately defined as a directory, since it directs you to something.

Other useful directories include:

- *Who's Who in America*—We've already looked at this series as a source of biographical information, but it is also a directory since it often provides contact information.
- *United States Government Manual*—This manuel provides contact information for government agencies and officials, in print and online (www.gpoaccess.gov/gmanual/index.html).

QUOTATION SOURCES: SAY WHAT?

Q: Who said the following:
  1) "The most beautiful thing we can experience is the mysterious. It is the source of all true art and science."
  2) "I learned three important things in college—to use a library, to memorize quickly and visually, and to drop asleep at any time given a horizontal surface and fifteen minutes. What I could not learn was to think creatively on schedule."
A:
  1) You may know this man by his more famous quote, "E=mc^2"—Albert Einstein.
  2) Agnes de Mille, the famous choreographer, in her book *Dance to the Piper*.
 Source:
  1) *Bartlett's Familiar Quotations*, 14th ed. (Boston: Little, Brown, 1968), 950.
  2) *The New York Public Library Book of 20th Century American Quotations* (New York: Warner Books, 1992), 165.

Books of quotations serve three purposes:

- to find quotes pertaining to a particular theme
- to find some quotes attributed to a particular person
- to find out who said something in particular

There are two basic varieties of quotation books: thematically arranged and chronologically arranged. The best-known book of quotations is *Bartlett's Familiar Quotations*, which belongs to the latter type although you can also find quotes on specific themes by looking up keywords in the index. Many such books group quotations together by author, making it possible to track down the statements of a given writer, regardless of their thematic content.

The source for the quotation from Agnes de Mille is a thematically arranged quotation book. Such compilations are great for finding a quote to use on a specific subject but not so useful in identifying the source of a quote.

BIBLIOGRAPHIES: WHERE DO I GO FROM HERE?

Q: How many children's books about President John Kennedy were published in the year following his assassination?
A: Nine children's books were published in 1964 alone, compared to only one in 1963. Source: Martin H. Sable, *A Bio-Bibliography of the Kennedy Family* (Metuchen, N.J.: Scarecrow Press, 1969).

Although you might think of a bibliography simply as the list of sources at the end of a book or journal article or as the list you must compile for your own research paper, there are also a wide variety of book-length bibliographies to be found in the typical reference room. These books can be enormously helpful because they are focused on one particular subject and provide citations for books, periodical articles, audiovisual material, and rare unpublished works relating to the subject.

As you can see, the reference room, whether real or virtual, is an oasis where your thirst for information can certainly be quenched. It is also a good place to prepare to be a contestant on "Who Wants to Be a Millionaire."

Evaluating Your Sources: The PACAC Method—Authority

WHO WROTE IT?
An author with credentials or some sort of track record adds credibility to a source. While you can't always find out much about the author, books often contain brief biographies. With periodicals, remember that you don't want to rely exclusively on popular magazines. Most articles from scholarly journals are not only written by experts in their field, they have often been selected by the author's peers as worthy of publication. If you're really interested in finding out more about authors, you can look them up on the Web (using the search engines that will be discussed in Chapter 7), or refer to such sources as *Who's Who* or *Contemporary Authors,* highlighted in this chapter.

When evaluating the authority of Web sites, remember that anyone can put up a Web site. Many sites have absolutely no editorial control. It is important to know who is behind the information that you see on a Web page, which can sometimes be more difficult than with print resources, since the author is not always identified. The 'Webmaster,' who may be named at the bottom of the page, is not necessarily the author; rather, this person designs or maintains the site.

You can tell a lot about a Web site simply from its address. As explained in Chapter 7, sites with domain names ending in .com are commercial sites. Such sites are usually trying to sell something; they are just advertising in disguise. Keep this fact in mind when evaluating the informational content of the site. If the domain name ends in .org, the site is put up by a nonprofit organization. Therefore, it is likely that the purpose of the site is to promote the cause of the organization. This bias will add a certain slant to the information. Sites affiliated with educational institutions have domain names ending in .edu. Although you might think that the information included in such sites would be free of propaganda, this is not a valid assumption. Also look out for students' personal pages. You can identify a personal page because its URL usually contains a tilde (~). The problem with such pages is that there is absolutely no editorial control. They may contain bad poetry, family photos, or a student's research paper. As previously mentioned, even government Web sites (those ending in .gov) can take a biased perspective and must be evaluated critically.

EXERCISES

For the ten questions below, identify the source you could use to find the answer by entering the appropriate letter in the space provided:

A) *Bartlett's Familiar Quotations,* B) *Timetables of History,* C) *United States Government Manual,* D) *Encyclopedia of Associations,* E) Biography Resource Center, F) *Encyclopedia of Religion,* G) Facts.com, H) *Statistical Abstract of the United States,* I) *Atlas of American History,* J) Britannica.com

1) ___ What type of animal is the most popular pet in the United States?
2) ___ Who is the director of the Society of Earthbound Extraterrestrials?
3) ___ What poem contains the line "Procrastination is the thief of time," and who wrote it?
4) ___ Which Olympic medals did world-champion figure skater Michelle Kwan win during her skating career?
5) ___ Is there any evidence that Mary Magdalene was really a prostitute?
6) ___ How does the evolutionary process of natural selection work?
7) ___ What other events happened in Europe at about the same time that Columbus discovered America?
8) ___ Where were the first and last battles of the Civil War fought?
9) ___ What specific functions does the Department of Homeland Security perform?
10) ___ When was the first successful circumnavigation of the earth in a balloon, how long did it take, and who accomplished this milestone?

Answers: 1) H, 2) D, 3) A, 4) E, 5) F, 6) J, 7) B, 8) I, 9) C, 10) G. Although you might find the answers to these questions in more than one of the sources listed, I have indicated the source that I would recommend first.

Six

Selecting Electronic Resources

Just as there are many makes and models of cars and the decision about which one to buy is often a difficult one, the range of resources available in your library or through your library's Web site is sometimes overwhelming. How do you know which databases to use? Fortunately, you don't have to pick just one, and you also don't have to spend any money to search them. But you can sure waste a lot of time if you use an inappropriate resource; you may never even find the information you need.

The cost and quality of the online databases highlighted in this chapter differentiate them from the free Web resources to be discussed in Chapter 7. In other words, when you search a Web-based periodical index or reference source, you are generally using a resource that has undergone a rigorous editorial process that enhances its quality and accuracy. Your library pays for the database and access is limited. There are exceptions, however. For example, government Web sites are excellent sources of authoritative information and many are freely accessible on the Web.

There are also some sites that provide free access to the indexing of articles but charge a fee for the full text. IngentaConnect (www.ingentaconnect.com), an extensive index to scholarly journals and books on a wide variety of subjects, is available free to anyone with access to the Web. Acquiring the articles, however, entails fees that can be somewhat hefty for college students struggling to pay for pizza and gas, not to mention textbooks. Google Scholar, from the makers of the search engine that has become so popular it is now used as a verb (as in 'to Google' someone), and Windows Live Academic Search (with the easy-to-remember address www.live.com) are two other indexes of articles and books that are free to search but charge a fee for the material. Then there is Questia (www.questia.com), a Web site that lets you search for articles and books for free, and even teases you with the text of the first page, but at the bottom of the screen displays the following message: 'Continue reading this publication now and get full access to Questia's entire online library with our no risk 7-day trial subscription.' For a permanent subscription you must pay $19.95 per month. These sites make you appreciate free services (and many free articles) offered by your academic or public library.

Usually, if a database is available for free on the Web, it is because the producer accepts advertising. For example, while searching for information about the *Titanic* on the Britannica Web site, which provides free access to the full text of 70 periodicals, you could click on the link 'Magazines' and get a list of article titles. Clicking on a title brings up the full text absolutely free. Your excitement will be somewhat short-lived, however, when you review the results. There certainly are quite a few articles, and some of them are from scholarly journals, but many of the articles are irrelevant, including quite a number from *Football Digest* about the Tennessee Titans, and *Science News* about Saturn's moon Titan. While searching through the list, a number of pop-up ads might appear, as well as continuous ads in the margin of the Web page advertising Britannica's products. It hardly seems worth the effort of closing all the pop-up ads or printing copies full of marginal ads, when you could get free copies of many relevant articles through the Web sites of practically any college library.

POPULAR ELECTRONIC RESOURCES

The rest of this chapter will describe the most popular online services in libraries and the databases they provide. Databases vary widely in details like how many periodicals each database indexes, how much full-text coverage is provided, or what years are included. Knowing what a given database contains is, of course, important, but here we will provide only a general overview. Instead, the subject focus of each source will be highlighted since that's the first step in deciding which databases to use.

There's really no need to read this chapter from beginning to end. One part of the exercises included at the end of the chapter is a checklist where you can identify those resources available through your library Web site. Focus on the databases you can access for now and make sure you read the descriptions pertaining to them. You can always refer back to this chapter if you encounter an unknown resource. As with the reference sources described in the previous chapter, not every library will have every one, but you should be able to access at least a few; if not, you can consult another library in your area including the local public library.

Before proceeding, it is important to understand that an online service usually provides access to a number of different subject-specific databases. InfoTrac, or the Thomson Gale Group, for example, is not one particular database, but the name of a service which includes a variety of resources. Think of an online service like a new car dealership; the individual databases provided are like the different car models. If you go to a Toyota dealer, you don't ask to see a Toyota; instead, you probably have specific models in mind, like a Corolla, Tercel, or Camry. In the same way, when you use InfoTrac, the Thomson Gale Group, or another online service, you need to select a specific database to search. The majority of databases available are periodical indexes, but there is also a wide variety of online reference sources.

Among different databases and database providers there is often overlap in what information is covered. An index like Expanded Academic ASAP, for example, covers many of the same periodicals as EBSCOhost's Academic Search, but there are certain titles that are unique to each of these databases. To offer another comparison, it's like going to a used-car lot. You may find some of the same car models at two or more different 'pre-owned' car dealers. But, if one dealer doesn't have exactly what you want, you simply go to another. The bottom line is that there is no single source to consult when researching your topic. You may have to go through a process of trial and error and search more than one database. In many cases, you can simultaneously search across multiple databases provided by a single company. This option can be a helpful way to save time, as you may be able to tell quickly which of the databases is providing you with the best results.

You will also find that some of the same databases are available through different online services. For example, an index to educational materials called ERIC, which is produced by the United States government, is accessible though EBSCOhost, FirstSearch, CSA, and Ovid, as well as through a government Web site. Although some online services produce the databases included in their collections, not all do. For example, Ovid produces no original material at all, but provides access to hundreds of resources produced by other companies. FirstSearch produces some of its databases but also provides access to databases it does not produce. The purpose shared by all online services we will look at is to provide access to databases, and each has its own unique interface for searching.

Thomson Gale InfoTrac

If your library has any of the databases produced by Thomson Gale, they provide some of the best places to start

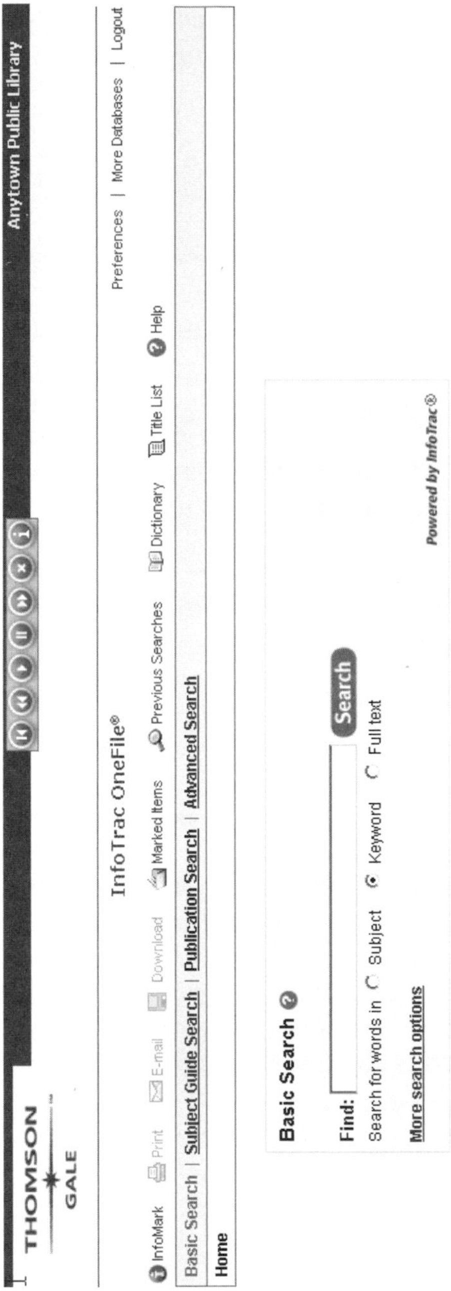

THOMSON
GALE

Anytown Public Library

InfoTrac OneFile®

Preferences | More Databases | Logout

InfoMark   Print   E-mail   Download   Marked Items   Previous Searches   Dictionary   Title List   Help

Basic Search | Subject Guide Search | Publication Search | Advanced Search

Home

Basic Search

Find:

Search for words in ○ Subject   ● Keyword   ○ Full text

Search

More search options

Powered by InfoTrac®

Figure 6.1: Opening search screen for InfoTrac OneFile.

your research. Some of the popular databases you are likely to encounter include:

- Expanded Academic ASAP—This index covers a wide selection of scholarly journals. The majority of journals indexed are peer-reviewed, so it's a good place to start college-level research.
- Biography Resource Center—This resource indexes biographical material and provides the full text from a variety of reference sources published by Gale as well as numerous periodicals.
- Business and Company Resource Center—This database indexes business magazines and trade journals.
- Gale Virtual Reference Library—This resource allows you to search the full text of hundreds of common reference sources.
- Health and Wellness Resource Center—This index covers medical and general health topics.
- InfoTrac Custom Newspapers—The newspapers covered by this full-text database are chosen by the subscribing library, so if your library has it, you should find the local papers from your area as well as the major national newspapers.
- InfoTrac OneFile—This database focuses on popular general-interest publications.
- Literature Resource Center—This database provides a combination of journal articles, literary criticism (including essays from *Contemporary Literary Criticism*), biographical information on authors, and literary reference works, including a comprehensive dictionary of literary terms. It also allows access to the *MLA International Bibliography*, which is the primary index for literary research. Note, though, that some institutions provide access to MLA through another publisher or service.
- Science Resource Center—Includes a combination of scientific reference sources, such as the *Gale Encyclo-*

pedia of Science and the *MacMillan Science Library,* and the full text of articles from journals, magazines, and newspapers on scientific topics.

EBSCOhost

EBSCOhost is similar to InfoTrac. This service provides access to a number of resources, including the Academic Search databases highlighted in Chapter 4 that are similar to Expanded Academic ASAP in content, covering a wide variety of subject areas. Your library might subscribe to the Complete, Elite, or Premier editions which differ only in the number of full-text titles provided. Among the other databases available through EBSCOhost are:

- Business Source—Produced by EBSCO, this database covers business magazines, and trade and academic journals, and also comes in Complete, Elite, and Premier editions.
- Newspaper Source—Besides indexing articles in leading national newspapers like the *New York Times*, the *Wall Street Journal*, *USA Today*, and the *Christian Science Monitor*, the text of over 100 local, regional, and international papers is included in this database, as well as newswires such as the Associated Press.
- Reference sources, including Columbia Granger's Poetry Database and Current Biography Illustrated.
- *MLA International Bibliography*—The primary index for literary research produced by the Modern Language Association.
- Readers' Guide Abstracts and many of the other periodical indexes published by the Wilson Company.

ProQuest

The ProQuest service provides access not only to its own databases, but to many published by other companies, such

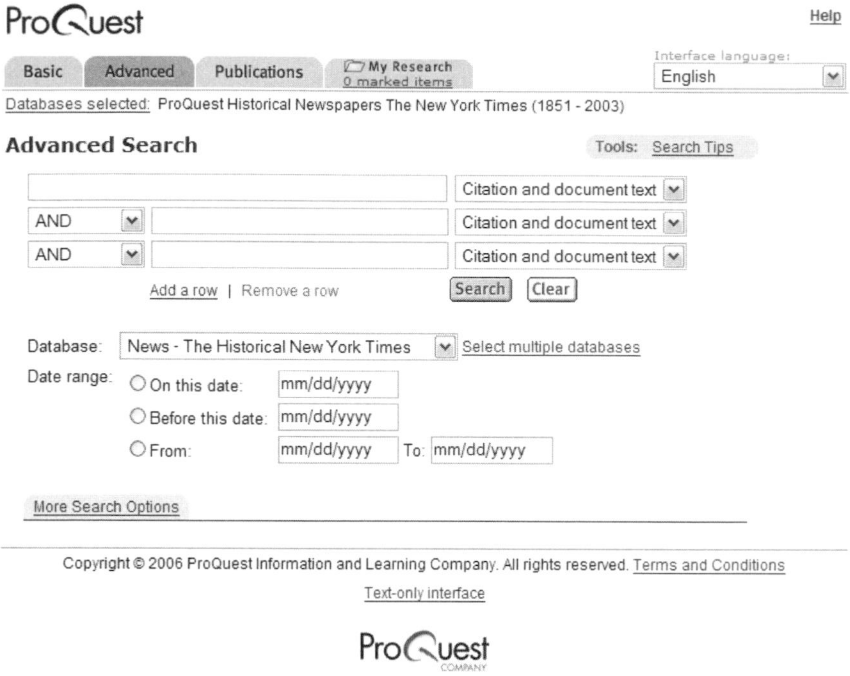

ProQuest

Basic	Advanced	Publications	My Research 0 marked items

Interface language: English

Databases selected: ProQuest Historical Newspapers The New York Times (1851 - 2003)

Advanced Search   Tools: Search Tips

	Citation and document text ✓
AND ✓	Citation and document text ✓
AND ✓	Citation and document text ✓

Add a row | Remove a row   [Search] [Clear]

Database: News - The Historical New York Times ✓ Select multiple databases

Date range: ○ On this date: mm/dd/yyyy

○ Before this date: mm/dd/yyyy

○ From: mm/dd/yyyy To: mm/dd/yyyy

More Search Options

Copyright © 2006 ProQuest Information and Learning Company. All rights reserved. Terms and Conditions

Text-only interface

ProQuest
COMPANY

Figure 6.2: Opening search screen for a ProQuest database.

as the Wilson subject indexes and MEDLINE. Among the popular ProQuest databases are:

- ProQuest Newstand—This resource indexes and abstracts the leading national and regional newspapers, including the *New York Times* and the *Wall Street Journal.* Your library might also subscribe to the separate ProQuest databases which provides the complete text of several major newspapers.
- ABI/INFORM—This index provides abstracts for business and management journals including many international journals. Libraries subscribe to the Global, Research, or Select editions. Trade & Industry, Dateline, and Archive databases are also available.

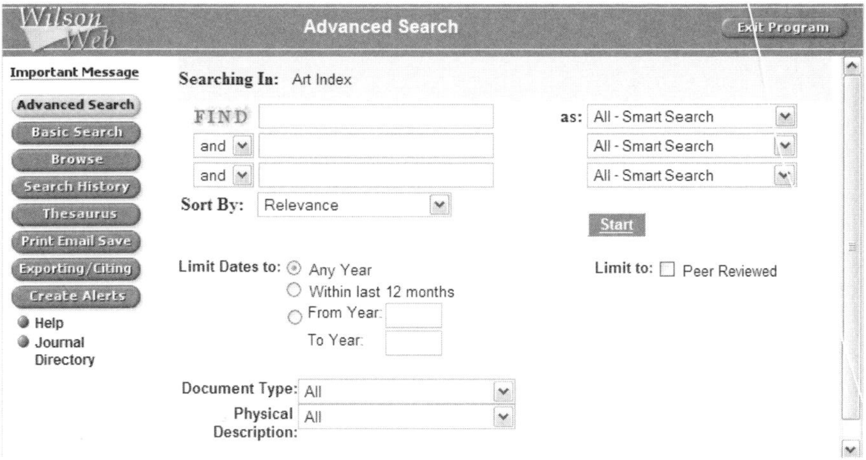

Figure 6.3 Opening search screen for *Readers' Guide* via WilsonWeb.

- ProQuest Research Library—This database covers journals, magazines, and newspapers on a wide variety of academic topics.
- ProQuest 5000—This resource is a combination of the databases already mentioned plus a number of others which together provide a good general reference database.
- ProQuest Platinum, Gold, and Silver—General coverage of a wide range of topics; Platinum indexes the most, followed by Gold, and then Silver.
- ProQuest Medical Library—This index covers all major medical journals.
- Periodicals Archive Online—This resource provides the full images of articles from a wide variety of journals from 1802 to 1995.
- ProQuest Historical Newspapers—This index goes back to the 19th century in its coverage.

WilsonWeb

The most well-known Wilson index is *Readers' Guide to Periodical Literature* which has been available in print since

1900. The H. W. Wilson Company has published subject-specific indexes in print for many years, and all of these indexes are now available in electronic versions. All of the indexes are available in Abstract and Full Text editions.

Wilson has its own online service, WilsonWeb, but Wilson databases are also available through EBSCOhost, FirstSearch, Ovid, and ProQuest. Wilson indexes are subject-specific, as indicated by the titles below.

- *Applied Science & Technology Index*—This database covers subjects relating to practical applications of science, including engineering, computers, telecommunications, transportation, and waste management. The Retrospective edition includes citations back to 1913.
- *Art Index*—Fine arts is the subject of this index. The Retrospective edition covers back to 1929.
- *Biography Reference Bank*—This database combines the information and indexing contained in all Wilson sources relating to biography. This includes Biography Index, which covers both periodicals and books about famous people, as well as biographical reference sources like Current Biography and World Authors 800 BC to Present. Your library might instead subscribe to Wilson Biographies Plus Illustrated, which provides the full text of all the biographical reference books that Wilson publishes but not the indexes.
- *Book Review Digest*—This resource includes excerpts from book reviews in popular review sources. The Retrospective edition covers back to 1905.
- *Education Index*—As the title implies, this index covers topics relating to education. The Retrospective edition covers back to 1929.
- *General Science Index*—This database indexes articles on topics related to pure science (as opposed to applied science and technology).
- *Humanities Index*—A variety of subjects is covered in this index, including literature and language, history,

philosophy, archaeology, classics, performing arts, history, and religion. The Retrospective edition covers back to 1907.

- *Readers' Guide to Periodical Literature*—This is the "classic" index covering a broad range of general topics. Readers' Guide Retrospective provides indexing for periodicals published all the way back to 1890.
- *Social Sciences Index*—This resource covers such topics as anthropology, area studies, economics, political science, psychiatry, psychology, social work and public welfare, sociology, urban studies, and women's studies. The Retrospective edition covers back to 1907.
- *Wilson Business Full Text*—General business magazines and trade journals are indexed by this database and the text of the articles is provided.
- *Wilson OmniFile*—This database combines the content of Education Index, General Science Index, Humanities Index, and Social Sciences Index with Wilson Business Full Text and Readers' Guide Full Text.

FirstSearch

FirstSearch, produced by an organization called OCLC (Online Computer Library Center), is primarily a service that provides access to the databases of other publishers. It currently gives library users access to more than 70 resources. This collection includes many of the Wilson databases, and other popular indexes such as MLA International Bibliography, ERIC, PsycINFO and MEDLINE. All of these databases can be easily searched using the FirstSearch interface.

Although the majority of databases included in FirstSearch is produced by other companies, OCLC does produce a very popular database called WorldCat which is like an online catalog for the world. With one search you can search online catalogs worldwide. More practically, if a book is not at your library, you can easily find out if it is at another area library without searching numerous catalogs. This

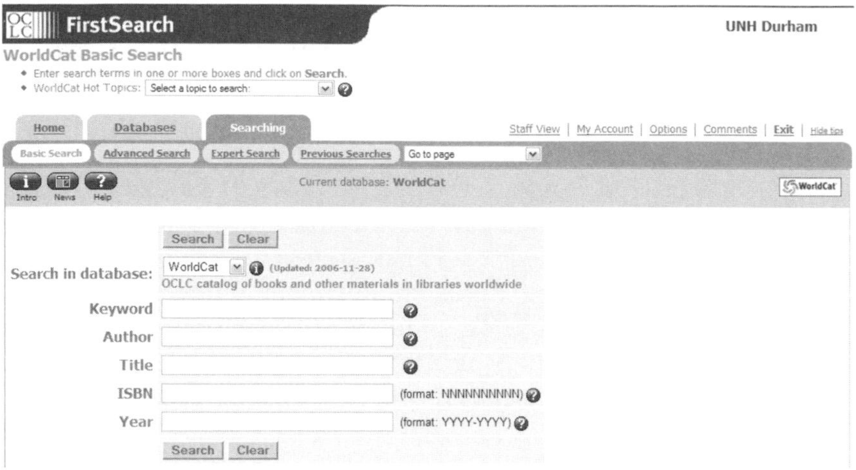

Figure 6.4: Opening screen for the FirstSearch database WorldCat.

database provides information not only on books, but also on a wide variety of nonbook material, including Web sites. You can enter a subject or keyword search and, by limiting your search to Internet files, retrieve a list of links to relevant sites. In this way, WorldCat serves as a very efficient search engine that retrieves highly relevant material. Because the sites included are assigned Library of Congress subject headings and are evaluated for quality, this database can be much more useful than the free Web search engines that retrieve a large proportion of irrelevant and low-quality resources. FirstSearch also includes ArticleFirst, a general index providing articles on a wide variety of subjects, and Electronic Collections Online, a full-text database of scholarly journals.

LexisNexis™ Academic

The emphasis of LexisNexis™ Academic, a database specifically geared toward the college audience, is on current news, business, legal, and medical topics, rather than on scholarly research. It provides access to the full text of thou-

Figure 6.5: Homepage of LexisNexis™ Academic.

sands of sources, including newspapers and magazines, world news services, newswire services, television transcripts, and federal and state laws and regulations. Many sources are updated daily. It is crucial to remember that the time period covered for publications may vary greatly. For example, the *New York Times* goes back to the 1980s, while the *Los Angeles Times* goes back a mere six months.

Ovid

Ovid Technologies does not produce any of its own databases, but they provide access to over 300 databases produced by other companies, such as Wilson, so you may use Ovid at your library to search some of the databases already described in this chapter. Among the more popular databases

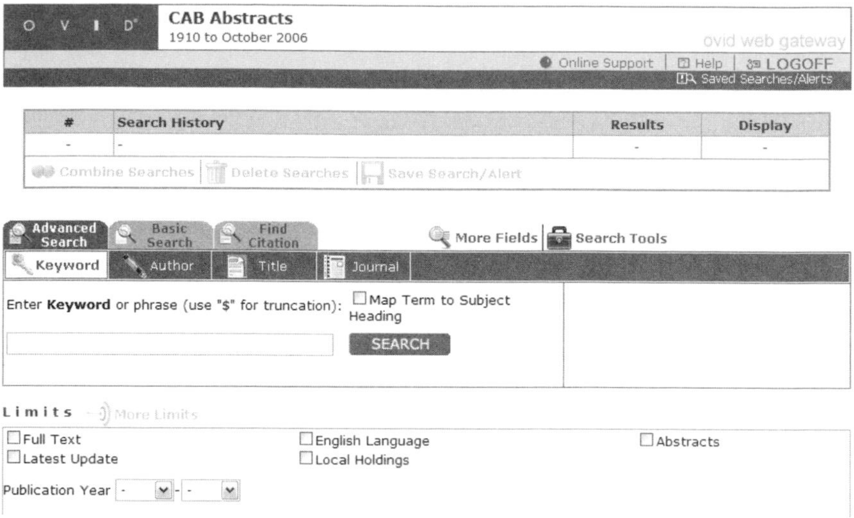

Figure 6.6: Opening search screen for an Ovid database.

provided to libraries by Ovid are PsycINFO, ERIC, and MEDLINE. Ovid also provides access to such reference sources as Who's Who and Peterson's College Guides. The service has some highly technical databases, like the Plant Protection Database and the Handbook of Injectable Drugs, that you probably won't need to use for typical college research papers.

CSA

CSA publishes and distributes over 100 bibliographic and full-text databases. These databases include a wide range of indexes in the areas of arts and sciences, natural sciences, social sciences, and technology.

JSTOR

JSTOR, short for 'journal storage,' is a database composed of journal articles exclusively in Portable Document Format

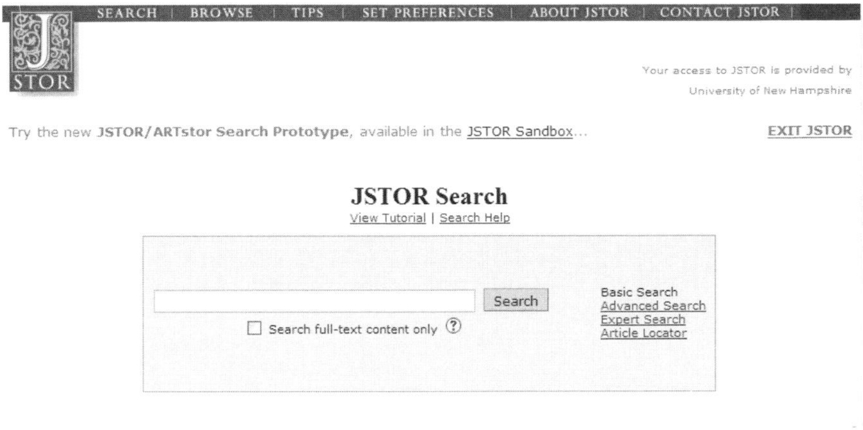

Figure 6.7: Opening search screen for JSTOR.

(PDF) format. The subjects covered by this resource are mainly related to the arts, humanities, social sciences, and natural sciences. While this is an essential resource, it is crucially important to note that JSTOR currently does not include articles from the past five to seven years. In some cases, this limitation has been extended out to the ten-year mark, limiting JSTOR's value to those needing up-to-the-minute coverage. Furthermore, while JSTOR's collection is huge, it rarely includes every major journal in a given field, and it does not include all fields.

NetLibrary

NetLibrary provides access to electronic versions of over 100,000 print books. These 'eBooks' include a variety of current popular works, scholarly titles, and older public domain materials. An individual library picks what eBooks it wants to rent for its customized collection, and then students can 'check out' these titles to read online. Once an eBook is checked out, it cannot be read by another library user until it is 'returned.' You can't print out the whole eBook, so you do have to read most of it on the screen. You can bookmark

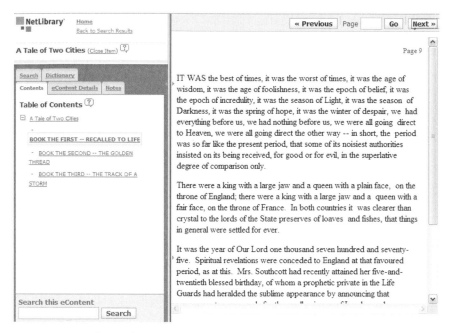

Figure 6.8: Sample page from a NetLibrary eBook.

pages and do something you would never do with a regular library book—write notes. These notes are saved in your personal account, to be viewed by you again if you check out the same title. Another nice feature is the ability to search the text of the book for a term, which is similar to looking up a subject in the index in the back of a regular book.

United States Government Databases

The United States government is one of the most prolific publishers in the world. Some of the popular databases already mentioned in this chapter are compiled by government agencies. For example, MEDLINE is the National Library of Medicine's database containing more than 13 million ar-

Figure 6.9: The National Library of Medicine's homepage providing free access to MEDLINE/PubMed.

ticles published in over 4,000 medical journals. Although MEDLINE is available via EBSCOhost, FirstSearch, Ovid, and other services, you can also access it for free by going to www.nlm.nih.gov and selecting PubMed. MEDLINE is the largest part of the PubMed database. MEDLINEPlus, also available from the NLM homepage, is a more con-sumer-oriented medical database.

ERIC is another database offered by various online ser-vices that can also be accessed at a government Web site. ERIC (Educational Resources Information Center) is sup-ported by the U.S. Department of Education and the Insti-tute of Education Sciences, and provides access to abstracts of over one million documents and journal articles concern-ing educational topics. It is available at www.eric.ed.gov.

Another important resource is the GPO Monthly Catalog, also known as the Catalog of United States Government

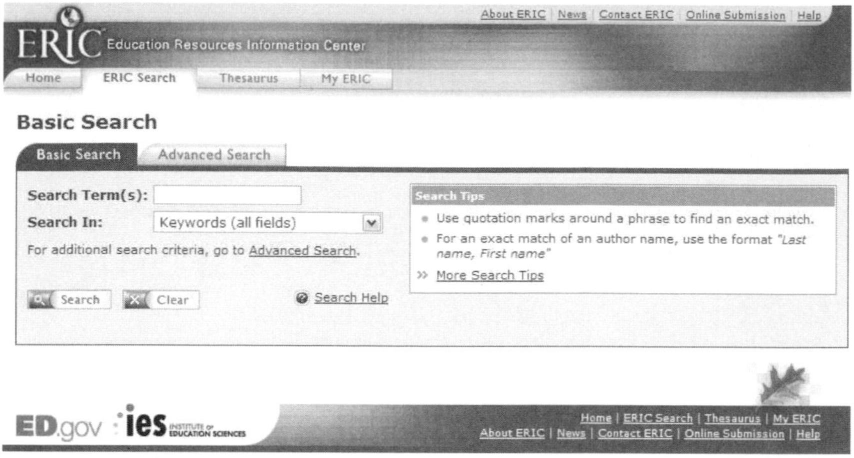

Figure 6.10: ERIC database basic search screen.

Publications, which indexes the publications of the Government Printing Office. While some of the publications indexed are available online, all can be obtained at any one of the numerous federal depository libraries throughout the country. To search this catalog, go to the GPO Access Web site at www.gpoaccess.gov, where you will also find an alphabetical listing of government resources available, ranging from the *9–11 Commission Report* to the *Weekly Compilation of Presidential Documents*.

There are certainly other databases that I have not covered here, but this book is not intended to turn you into a librarian. Being familiar with the major online services you are likely to encounter is sufficient and can help you understand the other lesser-known ones that may also be available in your library. Just as there are many different modes of transportation (cars, trucks, buses, trains, motorcycles, SUVs, and so forth), there are different resources for different research topics. Each serves a purpose, and each must be chosen with your particular needs in mind.

Figure 6.11: GPO Access Web site.

Evaluating Your Sources: The PACAC Method—Currency

WHEN WAS IT WRITTEN?

Sometimes it's important to have the most recent information available, especially for scientific and business-related topics. In such cases, as you search for material on your subject, you should keep in mind the date each item was written. This will help you to narrow your search and focus on the most valuable information. At other times, it is not necessary to have the most up-to-date material, particularly with historical topics or those related to the humanities. In fact, when researching such areas, the latest information may not be the best.

Most students, however, prefer more recent information, particularly periodical articles, because it is usually easier to obtain. Many older articles are on microfilm and to find citations for this material you may even have to use a print index rather than an electronic one. While full-text electronic sources are definitely convenient, don't rely exclusively on the sources available online. With the increasing availability of recent full-text articles online, more students are opting for current information. Fortunately, many information publishers are working to expand their backfiles online, making it much easier to obtain access to older materials.

It's easy enough to determine the date that a book was written. The copyright date will be on one of the first few left-hand pages. It will also be listed in the online catalog record. The dates for articles are included in the citations you found through indexes. Finding out how old a Web page is can be problematic (like so many things about the Web) because Web sites are constantly updated. If the Webmaster has followed the rules of good design and maintenance, the date when the site was last updated should appear prominently on the homepage as well as on each page that has been revised within the site. Even if a date does appear on a Web page, however, you often have no way of knowing if it is the date of initial creation or the date of most recent revision.

EXERCISES

1) In the following list of databases, subdivided by subject area, check off the ones that are available through your library's Web site. The online services through which these databases are available are indicated in parentheses. If more than one service is given, circle the one that provides the resource for your library. Make sure you read the descriptions of these databases and their providers included in this chapter.

General:
___ Academic Search (EBSCOhost)
___ ArticleFirst (FirstSearch)
___ Expanded Academic ASAP (InfoTrac)
___ Gale Virtual Reference Library (InfoTrac)
___ InfoTrac One File (InfoTrac)
___ ProQuest Research Library (ProQuest)
___ ProQuest 5000 (ProQuest)
___ ProQuest Platinum, Gold, and Silver (ProQuest)
___ Readers' Guide Abstracts (WilsonWeb, EBSCOhost, FirstSearch, Ovid)
___ Wilson Omni File (WilsonWeb, Ovid)
___ WorldCat (FirstSearch)

Biographical:
___ Biography Reference Bank (WilsonWeb)
___ Biography Resource Center (InfoTrac)
___ Wilson Biographies Illustrated (WilsonWeb, EBSCOhost)

Business:
___ ABI/INFORM (ProQuest, FirstSearch, Ovid)
___ Business and Company Resource Center (InfoTrac)
___ Business Source (EBSCOhost)
___ Wilson Business Abstracts (WilsonWeb, FirstSearch, Ovid)

Education:
___ Education Abstracts (WilsonWeb, EBSCOhost, FirstSearch, Ovid, ProQuest)
___ ERIC (EBSCOhost, FirstSearch, Ovid, Proquest)
___ Social Sciences Abstracts (Wilson, EBSCOhost, FirstSearch, Ovid, Proquest)

Humanities/Historical & Literature:
___ Art Abstracts (Wilson, EBSCOhost, FirstSearch, Ovid)
___ Book Review Digest (Wilson, EBSCOhost, FirstSearch, Ovid)
___ Humanities Abstracts (Wilson, EBSCOhost, FirstSearch, Ovid)
___ Literature Resource Center (InfoTrac)
___ MLA International Bibliography (EBSCOhost, FirstSearch, InfoTrac, Ovid, ProQuest)
___ JSTOR

Medical:
___ Health and Wellness Resource Center (InfoTrac)
___ MEDLINE (EBSCOhost, FirstSearch, Ovid, ProQuest)
___ PsycINFO (EBSCOhost, FirstSearch, Ovid, ProQuest)
___ ProQuest Medical Library (ProQuest)

Newspapers and Current Events:
___ InfoTrac Custom Newspapers (InfoTrac)
___ Academic Universe (Lexis-Nexis™)
___ GPO Monthly Catalog (FirstSearch)
___ Newspaper Source (EBSCOhost)
___ ProQuest Newstand (ProQuest)

Retrospective:
___ Periodicals Archive Online (ProQuest)
___ ProQuest Historical Newspapers (ProQuest)
___ Wilson retrospective indexes: Applied Science & Technology Index, Art Index, Book Review Digest,

Education Index, General Science Index, Humanities Index, Readers' Guide to Periodical Literature, Social Sciences Index

Science and Technical:
___ Applied Science & Technology Abstracts (Wilson, EBSCOhost, FirstSearch, Ovid, ProQuest)
___ General Science Abstracts (Wilson, EBSCOhost, FirstSearch, Ovid, ProQuest)
___ JSTOR
___ Science Resource Center (InfoTrac)

Other (list here any databases not included in this chapter that you think might be useful in your research):

_____

_____

_____

_____

2) List three of the databases checked above that you think will be most useful in finding information for your current paper topic:

_____

_____

_____

Seven

Navigating the World Wide Web

The cliché of the 'information superhighway' is hard to avoid when discussing the World Wide Web. There are ways in which this image is accurate and other ways in which it seems completely wrong. The Web certainly has the potential to provide the user with a wealth of quick information, but the reality is that it also has roadblocks of its own. The attitude of this chapter is, therefore, 'proceed with caution.' Don't rely on the Web alone for your research paper.

This chapter will only provide a brief introduction to the immensity of the World Wide Web. Entire books have been written about how to use the Web. These books quickly go out of date because the details they cover inevitably become obsolete. Similarly, the chapter about the Internet that appeared in the first edition of this book bears very little resemblance to this chapter. Therefore, my focus here will be on general principles that will probably not change too much rather than on the specifics that probably will.

THE STATE OF THE WEB

The terms 'World Wide Web' and 'Internet' are used almost interchangeably today, but the Internet came first. The Web can be considered as simply a way of using the Internet.

What we know as the Internet began in 1969 as the ARPANET project of the Department of Defense. What emerged from this project was a worldwide network of computers—an 'Internet.' Until the mid-1990s and the emergence of the Web, the Internet was a user-unfriendly system with no graphics. The unbelievable growth in the popularity of the Internet is due, in part, to the development of the Web as a graphical way of using this computer network.

The main problems with the Web are its disorganization, preponderance of useless information, and excessive advertising. Picture a big library where the material is not arranged by call number, but just sort of grouped together loosely by subject. This lack of organization can make it difficult to find the exact location of the material you need. Also, there are no librarians selecting items for quality; anything and everything is thrown in—elementary school compositions and high school book reports along with excerpts from doctoral dissertations and works by Pulitzer Prize–winning authors. In addition, you are bombarded with advertising as 'e-commerce,' rather than the sharing of knowledge, seems to emerge as the Web's reason for being. Web pages have widely divergent purposes: some are designed to sell something, persuade, educate, or serve any number of other functions.

A lot of what you find on the Web, is found accidentally. If you are looking for information on a particular topic, you can often become quite frustrated. Using the Web also presents technical problems. You may click on a link only to discover that a resource is not found or is no longer available. A Web site may be available one day and gone the next. Graphics may take a long time to load. Response time may also be slow because too many users are trying to access the same site. I don't mean to sound completely negative, however—I have found some wonderful information on the Web, and consider it, at its best, to be an amazing source of information.

THE STRUCTURE OF THE WEB

Think of the Web once again like a library full of books. Each Web site is like one book. Just as a book has a table of contents, a Web site has a homepage—an introductory page from which to begin your exploring. Although some sites may only be a single page and the book analogy doesn't really fit, most Web sites consist of more than one page. Your school's homepage probably allows you to connect to all the different departmental pages, as well as pages about events, services, and the library. A page is a misleading term because the Web does not confine the designer of a Web site to a certain amount of space. Pages can be of all different lengths. A page on the Web is defined as the space that you can scroll through at a particular address.

In addition to providing information, most Web pages also contain links to other Web pages. You can access other pages by clicking on these hypertext links. Links can be either highlighted text or a graphical image. To extend our book metaphor, let's say you're looking in a book for information on your topic. You could read the book from cover to cover in a linear fashion, or you could check the index in the back of the book to determine which pages contain the specific information you need and then turn to those pages. While looking in the index, you might see related topics listed with their appropriate page numbers. Referring to these different pages and flipping back and forth in a book using the index is what hypertext is all about. But the Web takes it a step further. Imagine looking in the bibliography at the end of a book and instantly being able to get your hands on some of the sources cited. This is the sort of thing that Web page links allow you to do.

You use browsing software to view Web sites. Popular browsers include Firefox, Internet Explorer, Safari, Opera, and Netscape. The same Web page might look slightly different if viewed from two computers using different browsing software. Yet, just as two editions of a book might look different but contain exactly the same text, the content of the Web site remains the same. (Note: the screenshots displayed throughout this book were all viewed with Internet Explorer.)

THE CONTENT OF THE WEB

In contrast to most of the other Web-based sources in this book, the Web resources that are the focus of this chapter are freely accessible to anyone who has access to the Web. In a figurative sense, no toll is required. As with just about anything that appears to be free, however, there are often hidden costs in the form of advertising and propaganda.

What can you find on the Web? That's like asking what you can see on a cross-country road trip. Because of the sheer bulk of information available, only some broad generalizations can be offered here based on the categories of information providers.

- **Companies** provide a lot of information about their products and services on the Web. Mostly it is just advertising, but sometimes such information can be helpful. If you're researching a company, you will certainly want to take a look at its Web site. Many commercial sites are not only sources of information but interactive sites where customers can purchase products and perform transactions.
- **Nonprofit organizations** also have a strong presence on the Web. These organizations are formed to promote a cause, so their sites are designed to help in their mission. No matter how altruistic this mission is, watch out for propaganda and bias when viewing these sites. They're certainly not out to make a buck the way the commercial sites blatantly are, but they often have an agenda.

- **Educational Institutions**—just about every college and university has a Web site. Many secondary and elementary schools have their own sites as well. Access to your library's Web-based resources is usually provided through your school's site. In addition to lots of information about events, student services, courses, and individual departments, colleges often let students and faculty post their own personal pages. While these Web pages can be excellent sources for research, be careful to evaluate the material using the PACAC method. You might have at your disposal the wisdom of a world-renowned expert in Shakespearean studies who has made his research available to the world with no thought of financial gain. Or, at the other end of the spectrum, you might be able to view a fraternity site that explains how to make your own beer. Additionally, librarians at many academic institutions work hard to identify Web sites they think will be useful to their students, staff, and faculty.
- **U.S. government departments and agencies** have always had a strong presence in cyberspace, ever since the Internet originated back in the late 1960s as a project of the Department of Defense. As mentioned in Chapter 5, government Web sites can be wonderful, objective sources of information and provide lots of statistics, reports, and so on, though you should remember to think critically about any information you find on them.
- **Personal Web** sites can often be the biggest offender in the amount of junk on the Web. A subset of this category, Web logs or "blogs," are basically Web-based personal diaries, and have grown immensely in popularity over the past couple of years. Some, such as the Huffington Post (www.huffingtonpost.com) and Daily Kos (www.dailykos.com) have come to be quite influential even with those in the traditional media. You can often recognize a personal Web site by the presence of

a tilde (~) in the address. Although the other categories of sites usually have some form of editorial control because there is a higher organization to which the Web page author has to answer, personal pages can contain anything from pornography to cookie recipes. Another type of site in this category is the "wiki" which is a site that can be altered by anyone. Wikipedia (www. wikipedia.org), for example, an online encyclopedia containing articles on a wide range of topics, can be edited by anyone, expert or not, who wants to add, delete, or correct something from an article. Jimmy Whales, the creator of Wikipedia, has said that the site shouldn't be used as a scholarly source. While the site has mechanisms in place to police controversial topics, incorrect information can still sneak into even the best articles. Be extremely cautious when using personal sites, and make sure that the original source of any secondary information is clearly cited.

FINDING INFORMATION ON THE WEB

Web Addresses

Addresses, also called URLs or 'uniform resource locators,' are entered in the location box of your browser in order to access a particular Web page. These addresses often begin with 'www,' but entering these characters is no longer required. You also see Web addresses that begin with 'http://,' but you can omit this when entering the URL. The domain name, the first part of the address that takes you to a homepage, ends with one of the following codes (called top-level domains) that give an indication of the source of the information:

- **.com**—commercial sites; two other commercial top-level domains are **.pro**, for doctors, lawyers, and accountants, and **.biz**.

- **.org**—nonprofit organizations; the specific top-level domain **.museum** is reserved for—you guessed it—museums.
- **.edu**—educational institutions.
- **.gov**—government agencies; the related top-level domain **.mil** specifies a military site.
- **.net**—Internet service providers, which are companies that provide access to the Web; personal Web sites often have this top-level domain.
- **.name**—a top-level domain for personal Web sites.
- **.info**—a general top-level domain for individual sites, businesses, or organizations.

The address for a Web page is equivalent to the call number for a book and is often structured hierarchically like a call number. If you know the address, you can easily find the source. You can obtain Web site addresses from a variety of sources—magazines, books, TV commercials, librarians, professors, friends, acquaintances, and so on. Specific addresses for pages in a Web site beyond the homepage are lengthier and often more complicated, with backslashes to separate each portion of the URL. For example, suppose you wanted a recap of the first episode of *Lost* from the show's second season. While the address for the ABC network homepage is http://abc.go.com, the specific address for the page providing information on season two's premier show is http://abc.go.com/primetime/lost/episodes/223.html, probably not an address you would know off the top of your head, just as you wouldn't know a call number by heart. You are more likely to get to this page by clicking on links within the ABC site.

Surfing

Surfing is basically a process of clicking on Web page links. To get to the *Lost* episode page just mentioned:

Odyssey (CM-109) and Aquarius (LM-7)

Mission Objective:

Apollo 13 was supposed to land in the Fra Mauro area. An explosion on board forced Apollo 13 to circle the moon without landing. The Fra Mauro site was reassigned to Apollo 14.

Launch:

Saturday, April 11, 1970 at 13:13 CST.

At five and a half minutes after liftoff, Swigert, Haise, and Lovell felt a little vibration. Then

---

Figure 7.1: A portion of a page from NASA's Web site. (Available: http://science.ksc.nasa.gov/history/apollo/apollo–13/apollo–13.html.)

- Click on the link 'Shows,' which brings up a list of programs
- From this list select 'Lost,' which brings up a page dedicated to the show
- Click on 'Recaps,' which brings up a page that asks you to select a season
- After choosing 'Season 2,' you will see a summary of the first episode as well as links to all the other episodes aired that season

Clicking on four links is all it took to get from the homepage to the specific page you wanted.

You are not restricted, however, to surfing within one Web site. For example, take a look at Figure 7.1, a page from NASA's Web site which gives a brief history of the ill-fated Apollo 13 mission.

Notice in the second line under 'Mission Objective' that the word 'moon' is highlighted. When you click on this highlighted term, you can immediately access a Web site with information about the moon, as displayed in Figure 7.2. This Web site has nothing to do with NASA; it's maintained by

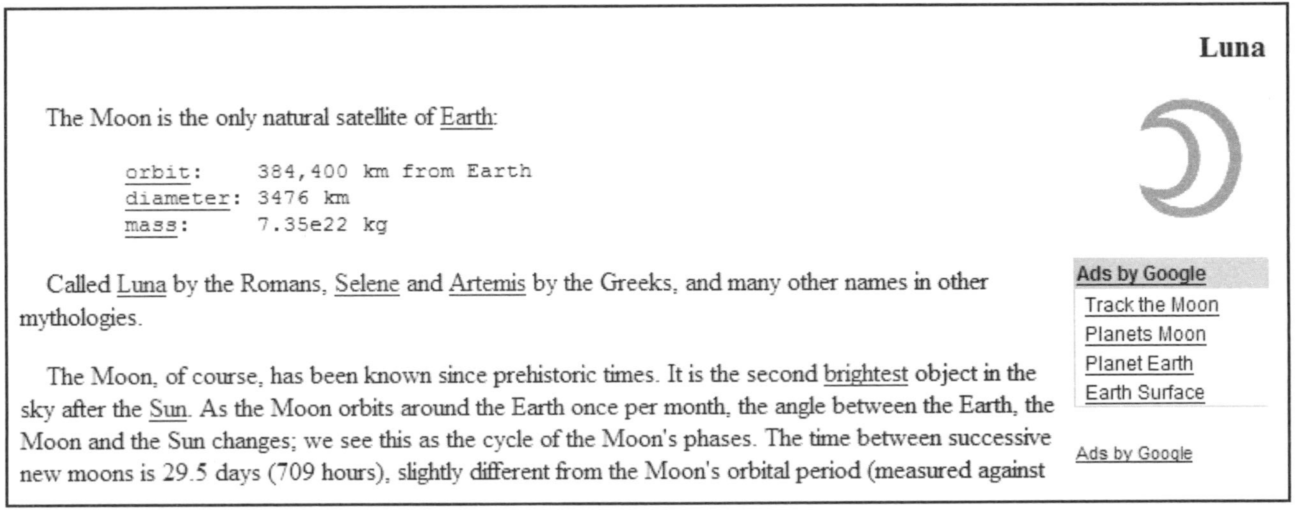

Luna

Ads by Google

Track the Moon
Planets Moon
Planet Earth
Earth Surface

Ads by Google

The Moon is the only natural satellite of Earth:

```
orbit:     384,400 km from Earth
diameter:  3476 km
mass:      7.35e22 kg
```

Called Luna by the Romans, Selene and Artemis by the Greeks, and many other names in other mythologies.

The Moon, of course, has been known since prehistoric times. It is the second brightest object in the sky after the Sun. As the Moon orbits around the Earth once per month, the angle between the Earth, the Moon and the Sun changes; we see this as the cycle of the Moon's phases. The time between successive new moons is 29.5 days (709 hours), slightly different from the Moon's orbital period (measured against

Figure 7.2: A portion of a page from "The Nine Planets: A Multimedia Tour of the Solar System," by Bill Arnett. (Available: http://seds.lpl.arizona.edu/nineplanets/nineplanets/luna.html.)

a software engineer named Bill Arnett who lives in Arizona and is interested in astronomy.

From this site, if you click on the name 'Artemis,' which is highlighted, you'll be taken to another Web site at an altogether different location that discusses Greek mythology. This is the nature of hypertext and what makes the Web so enticing. Although it gives you the freedom to jump around and follow various topics that may only have loose connections, it's really just like wandering around a library that isn't organized very well and haphazardly opening up books.

Search Engine Overview

Web sites that are specifically designed to help you find other sites are called 'search engines.' Using search engines to find Web sites can be loosely compared to using an online catalog to find books. The purpose of this section is not to explain how to use each one. That would be quite futile considering how much they change, and also impossible considering the sheer number of them. There are thousands of search engines listed at www.searchengineguide.com. But you should understand the common features that the major search engines share, as well as some of the unique features that distinguish them. Table 7.1 gives you an overview of the major search engines and other Web-based tools that help you find sites. To find out the latest developments and news about search engines go to www.searchenginewatch.com.

Despite the variety of search engines, they all provide a search box in which you can enter your terms, and, in return, get a list of links to sites that contain these terms. Unfortunately, most search engines are becoming so filled with shopping guides and other commercial material that it's hard to know exactly what to do once you get to one of them. The search box almost gets lost in the screen as the user is enticed by a variety of consumer links and services like e-mail, chat, horoscopes, and personal ads. Search engines that incorporate a variety of resources and services, including

Table 7.1: Selected Tools for Searching the Web.

About (www.about.com)—Searches sites chosen by over 500 expert human "guides."

Ask.com (www.ask.com)—Formerly AskJeeves, this search engine utilizes ExpertRank technology to improve the relevancy of sites found.

Dogpile (www.dogpile.com)—A meta-search engine that simultaneously searches most popular search engines including MSN Search, Ask.com, Google, and Yahoo!

Google (www.google.com)—This most popular search engine that covers billions of pages has a very sophisticated relevancy ranking technology that ranks, in part, by popularity and yields excellent results; no pay-for-placement is allowed.

Infomine (http://infomine.ucr.edu/)—This Web directory covers scholarly resources.

Librarians' Internet Index (www.lii.org)—Over 20,000 sites carefully chosen by librarians are included in this Web directory.

MSN Search (http://search.msn.com)—This is Microsoft's popular search engine.

Open Directory (http://dmoz.org)—Over four million sites are indexed by this directory compiled by volunteer editors.

WWW Virtual Library (www.vlib.org)—This is an advertising-free directory of the Web compiled by volunteers who are experts in a wide range of subject areas.

Yahoo! (www.yahoo.com)—One of the oldest directories on the Web, Yahoo! has become increasingly commercial over the past few years.

Web directories, free e-mail, news, chat rooms, and online shopping, are called 'portal sites.' The emphasis of these portals seems to be on commercial purposes rather than academic research. The opportunities to buy things, chat with people, and check out the latest news can be very distracting on such sites as Yahoo!, About.com, and Lycos.

In contrast to such distracting arrays, take a look at the uncluttered Google homepage displayed in Figure 7.3.

Advertising does appear on Google search result pages, but these links to sponsor sites are text only and very unobtrusive. Google, with its often relevant results and low-key advertising, has become the most popular search engine. Google is a portal site providing a variety of services, some of which are listed on the homepage above the search box, including Froogle, which is a shopping site. If you click on 'more,' you will see a listing of all of Google's services. Although many of them are consumer-oriented (like Catalogs and Checkout) or communication-related (like Blogger and Gmail), one that may be helpful in your research is Google Scholar, which searches for scholarly literature. This last resource is a helpful addition to the Google family, ranking search results according to the relevance of the full text, publication, and so on in the attempt to provide the most relevant resources. But at present the range of publications covered and the scope of materials indexed is relatively limited, meaning that this service should not take the place of databases licensed by libraries.

Search Engine Directories

Although I compared search engines to online book catalogs, there is a major difference. Records in an online catalog have a standard format and are assigned subject headings, which makes it easy to access all items on a certain topic once you have determined what the appropriate headings are. But you generally enter keywords in search engines; as always, this

Figure 7.3: Google homepage.

means that your searching will be imprecise. OCLC's WorldCat, a FirstSearch database described in Chapter 6, has begun cataloging Web sites just as it does books and other material, in an attempt to create an online catalog for the Web that classifies sites using Library of Congress subject headings.

To provide a way to access sites by subject, many search engines have directories that arrange sites hierarchically into various categories. Thus you can browse if your topic is fairly broad, rather than entering keywords in the search box. This design is as close as search engines come to assigning subject headings to sites.

Most of the major search engines, including Google, integrate the Open Directory Project (ODP) into their site to provide the directory listings. The Open Directory Project (http://dmoz.org) categorizes over four million Web sites under a small number of main headings listed in its directory. The homepage of this directory is displayed in Figure 7.4.

Clicking on one of ODP's main headings will bring you to another page that lists the subheadings for the chosen topic. For example, let's say you wanted to find a list of Web sites that provide TV theme-song lyrics. Clicking on the first category in the directory, 'Arts,' brings up the screen displayed in Figure 7.5.

From this screen select 'Television.' The next screen to appear is shown in Figure 7.6, which lists narrower subheadings, including 'Theme Songs.'

Click on 'Theme Songs' and you will see the listing of individual sites, as displayed in Figure 7.7.

What Are You Searching?

At this point it is important to understand that no search engine covers the entire Web. Even metasearch engines like MetaCrawler and Dogpile that allow you to search multiple engines simultaneously, don't cover every single page. Each engine covers a different range of sites just as each online catalog covers a different collection of resources, but there is definitely overlap among search engines, just like there is overlap among periodical indexes.

There are two ways that search engines select the sources to be covered. Sites can be evaluated by human beings for inclusion in a directory. Yahoo!, for example, employs a team of people to find acceptable sites and then assign a category to each one. Yahoo! also accepts user submissions, which are evaluated by their team for inclusion. Search engines that allow you to search outside the limited scope of a human-compiled subject directory automate the whole process of selection by sending out electronic 'spiders' that 'crawl' to sites and add them to the database. Then the spiders follow all the links on the initial sites and add all of those secondary sites, and so on. Some search engines that

Figure 7.4: Open Directory Project homepage.

boast the number of pages they index rely on quantity rather than quality. This difference is important when it comes to evaluating the results of your search.

The lesson to be learned is that if your topic is somewhat broad, you might want to use a search engine's directory that covers fewer sites and employs some selection criteria. On the other hand, if your topic is a bit more obscure, you may want to start by entering keywords in the search box. It is also important to work with more than one search engine, so that potentially worthwhile materials don't slip through the net of a given search engine's coverage.

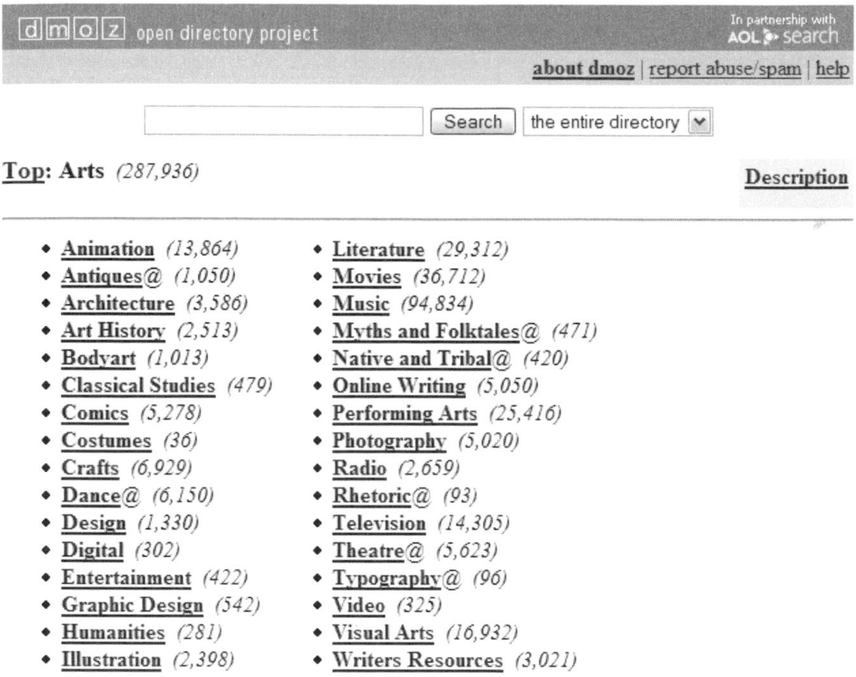

Figure 7.5: Open Directory Project's "Arts" directory.

Searching Techniques

Much of what you learned about searching a database in Chapter 2 relates to searching the Web, so I won't give a lot of examples in this section. Each search engine is a little different. Most have help pages that provide you with tips and examples to highlight their unique features. Like just about all the databases we've seen in this book, there are both basic and advanced ways of using Web search engines, but typically the average search user never gets beyond entering a string of keywords in the search box and then browsing through a list of links that can often contain irrelevant sites.

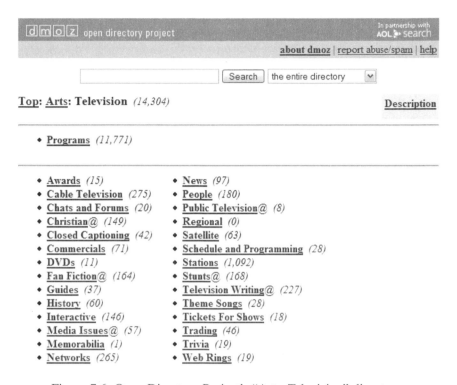

Figure 7.6: Open Directory Project's "Arts: Television" directory.

First of all, you can use Boolean connecting terms in most Web search engines. The ways in which you do this differ from engine to engine. But generally, if you enter a string of keywords, the connector AND is implied between them in most of the major search engines. So the more keywords you enter, the fewer results you will get and the more precise your search will be. Because AND is implied, an almost universal rule is that, in order to find an exact phrase, you enter it within quotation marks (some search engines allow you to select "exact phrase" as an option on the advanced search screen). If you were to enter **Faith Hill** in a search engine without quotation marks, you would retrieve all the sites that contain the words 'faith' and 'hill,' so some of

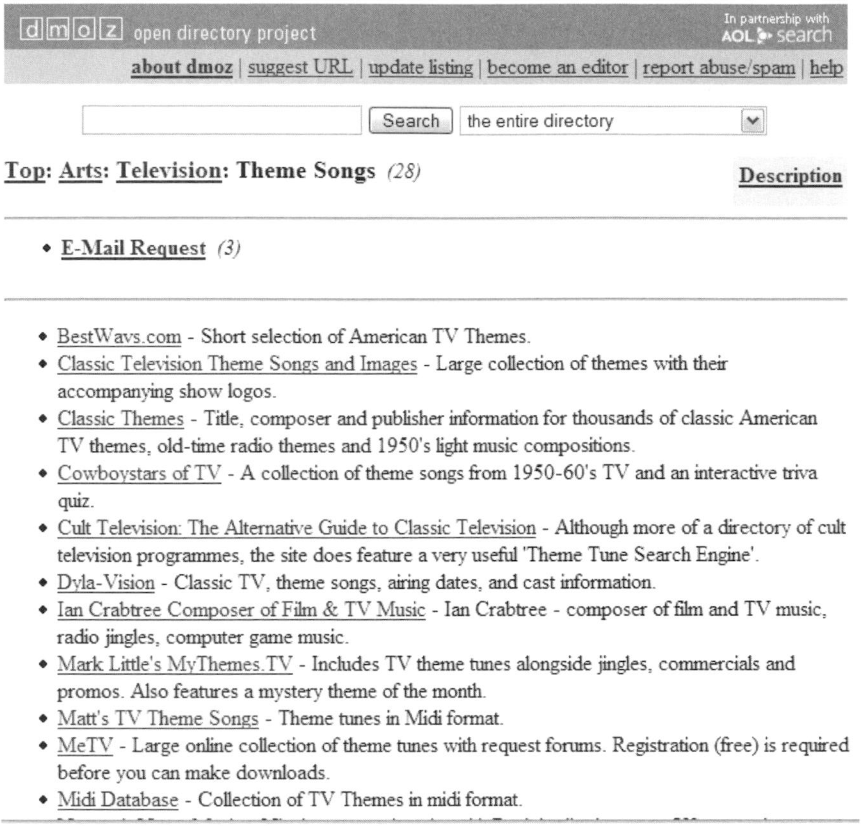

Figure 7.7: Open Directory Project's "Arts: Television: Theme Songs" directory.

these sites would be irrelevant including a number relating to mountains and the bible.

You can also use the connector OR to broaden your search in most search engines. Some search engines, such as Ask.com, consider *or* a keyword rather than a connecting term unless it is entered in capital letters, so enter **OR** rather than **or**. Not all Web search engines support truncation, so if you want to find the variant endings of a search term and are not sure if truncation works, just enter all variations of the word connected by **OR**.

The minus sign (-) signifies NOT in some search engines, eliminating a term from your search. For example, if you entered **'Pirates of the Caribbean'-'Johnny Depp'** in just about any of the search engines, you will increase your chances of finding sites concerned with the Disney ride rather than Johnny Depp fan club sites and other sites concerned with the swashbuckling movie. Conversely, the plus sign (+) indicates that a term must be found, which is most useful when you need to find words that the search engine usually ignores, such as prepositions ('at,' 'to,' 'from,' and so on) and other short words (including 'where,' 'what,' 'that').

Most search engines have an advanced search page that facilitates the searching process. As you can see in Figure 7.8, Google provides a more detailed search form that simplifies Boolean searching by letting you find sites 'with **all** of the words' (AND), 'with the **exact phrase**,' 'with **at least one** of the words' (OR), or '**without** the words' (NOT). It also lets you limit your search by language and date updated, and allows you to specify where you want the terms to occur (for example, in the title of the Web page, which can help retrieve more relevant sites, or anywhere in the page, which will increase your results).

How Web Search Engines Rank Results

When you do a keyword search in an online catalog, your list of books is usually displayed in alphabetical or date order. When you receive a list of Web site links in response to your search engine query, what order are they displayed in? Some search engines employ a relevancy ranking that orders sites retrieved by the frequency of search terms. In other words, sites that contain all of your words in the greatest quantity will appear at the top of the list. Other search engines rank sites by popularity so that the sites which have been visited the most by other users on this topic will appear first. The reasoning is that the most useful sites will emerge since users have, in a way, voted for them.

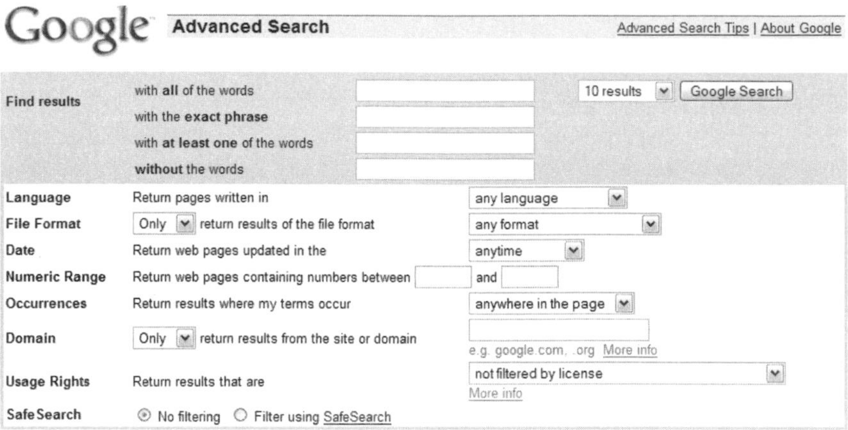

Figure 7.8: Google advanced search page.

To prevent deliberate exploitation by Web site designers who might want to improve their sites' ranking, the searching and ranking algorithms of search engines are not transparent or readily available. For example, we know that Google employs a variation of the popularity method, which has proven to be highly effective in retrieving relevant sites. Sites that are linked to the most by other sites have a higher ranking. For example, if you search for John F. Kennedy, the first site in the results list is a biography of Kennedy at the White House's Web site. This means that more sites about Kennedy link to www.whitehouse.gov than to any other site. The logic here is that a site that has been chosen by the designer of another site to be included as a link must be a useful site.

Then there is a deceptive type of ranking which is linked to fees that Web sites pay to search engines. For example, Yahoo! allows companies to pay a fee so that their sites will appear more prominently than others. These 'pay-for-placement' sites may not be as useful in your research as noncommercial sites.

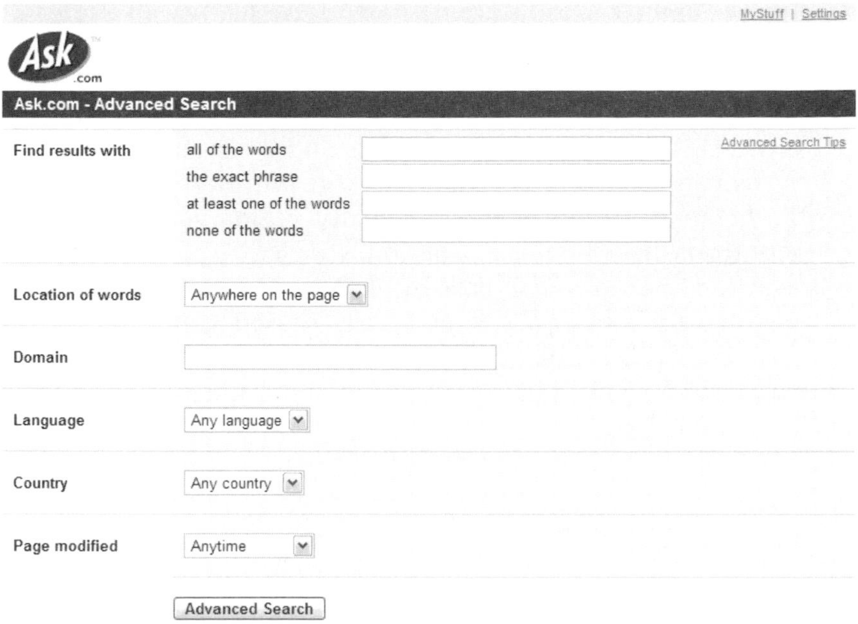

Figure 7.9: Ask.com advanced search page.

Search Engine Recommendations

In previous editions of this book, Yahoo! was recommended for subjects of a general nature, but this search engine, among the first to emerge when the Web came into existence, has become increasingly commercial. It is now more appropriate to search Yahoo! for subjects of a more practical nature, such as making travel plans, or after using other search engines. Right now, Google seems to be all the rage, but with the ever-changing nature of the Web, another upstart could take its place. You will develop your own personal favorites based on your success rate and your comfort level. It's best to choose a couple of search engines that you like—perhaps one for broad searches and one for narrower topics—and focus on learning how to use them well. Refer again to Table 7.1, earlier in this chapter, for a list of the major search engines and other tools for finding Web sites.

You may find Web sites with pages that are 'Under Construction.' In a way, the entire Web is under construction, and by its nature, it will always be a work in progress, just as the highway system must continually be maintained, with new roads being built and old ones paved over. The tools used to search the Web are also under construction. So, be prepared for a bumpy ride and, as I advised you in the beginning of this chapter, proceed with caution. But enjoy the ride because you will certainly see some unexpected and wonderful things.

Evaluating Your Sources: The PACAC Method—Accuracy

IS THE INFORMATION CORRECT?

Accuracy is related to content and is most applicable to evaluating Web sites. A book or article should have gone through an editorial process which includes fact checking. On the other hand, I'm sure it is clear by now that Web sites are often unedited, and as a result they can contain a lot of erroneous information. But print resources are not perfect either. If you have found a number of articles and books and gained a working knowledge of your subject, you may have learned enough to notice inaccuracies in some of your print resources too. If you detect numerous inaccuracies in a resource, you may want to reconsider using it.

You should be cautious even if you notice minor errors like misspellings, because they reflect poorly on the source as a whole. Here's an example that points out the weakness of the Web as compared to edited print sources. I always thought that gardeners were more likely to get warts because I had heard about 'planters warts.' Maybe that's why I never strived to have a 'green thumb.' But gardening does not cause this condition—the correct spelling is 'plantar warts.' Plantar refers to the sole of the foot and has nothing to do with plants. Using the search engine Ask.com, I looked up the term 'plantar warts' and found 44,600 Web pages. Then I misspelled the term 'planters warts' and still found 6,350! That's a pretty bad error rate; one out of every eight Web pages on the topic misspelled it as 'planters warts.' The search of Ask.com turns up mostly .com sites. If you are looking for an authoritative source, such as the Mayo Clinic, you may have to search for quite a while. Contrast this with a search of MEDLINE, an index that covers medical journals. Not a single record misspelled the term 'plantar warts.' Indexes like MEDLINE also help guarantee that search results will be informative rather than merely commercial. For instance, MEDLINE lists the Mayo Clinic, as well as several other reputable consumer health sites, in the first few hits.

EXERCISES

1) Which Web site would be the best choice if you needed to find a few carefully reviewed noncommercial sites about hybrid cars?

   a) Google
   b) Open Directory
   c) Yahoo!
   d) About.com

2) Which Web site would be the best choice if you wanted to search several popular search engines simultaneously?

   a) Ask.com
   b) Librarians' Internet Index
   c) WWW Virtual Library
   d) Dogpile

3) All of the following Web sites are advertising-free except:

   a) MSN Search
   b) Open Directory
   c) Librarians' Internet Index
   d) WWW Virtual Library

4) Which Web site would be the best choice if you wanted to find a lot of links to other sites about dust devils (little sand-filled desert tornados)?

   a) Yahoo!
   b) About.com
   c) Google
   d) Open Directory

5) Which Google search would be the best way to retrieve links to sites about dust devils in Arizona?

    a) Arizona dust devils
    b) Arizona dust devil tornado
    c) 'Arizona dust devil tornado'
    d) Arizona 'dust devil' tornado

Answers: 1) b, 2) d, 3) a, 4) c, 5) d. Choice **a** also retrieves sites about various sports teams and choice **c** finds nothing with that exact phrase. Choices **b** and **d** will both find relevant sites but **d** is more precise because dust and devil must be found together as a phrase.

Eight

Preparing a Flawless Bibliography

The end product of your research is the paper or project that you complete for your class. This book is not intended to teach you how to write the paper, but an important component of your paper is the documentation that gives credit to the sources you used to write it. Because students frequently ask librarians how to cite sources, a discussion of the basics of citation certainly falls within the scope of this book.

There is no single method of citing sources. Your professor may request that you follow Chicago style (or Turabian, which is its simplified version). Two other common formats are MLA (Modern Language Association) style and APA (American Psychological Association) style. No matter which style you choose, the important thing is to be consistent. In other words, if you use MLA style for one citation, you must use MLA for all. To learn how to use these styles more thoroughly than discussed here, refer to the following handbooks available in most libraries:

- *The Chicago Manual of Style* (see Chapter 15)
- *A Manual for Writers of Term Papers, Theses, and Dissertations,* by Kate Turabian
- *The MLA Handbook for Writers of Research Papers*
- *The Publication Manual of the American Psychological Association* (APA)

Each of these four books will show you in great detail how to cite just about anything you could possibly want to cite. More recent editions include rules on citing electronic resources.

A number of Web sites also provide guidelines on citations:

- Citation Machine (http://citationmachine.net) is an interactive site that generates an MLA or APA style citation after you enter information about the source.
- Long Island University maintains a site providing examples of all of the major styles (www.liu.edu/CWIS/ CWP/library/workshop/citation.htm).
- The Writing Center at the University of Wisconsin-Madison has a good guide to Chicago style (www.wisc.edu/writing/Handbook/DocChicago.html).

The list of sources that you include at the end of your paper is generically referred to as a bibliography. If you're using the Chicago style, just call it the 'Bibliography.' When using MLA style, however, you title this page 'Works Cited,' while according to APA, it is called 'References.' In addition to providing a bibliography, you need to incorporate notes into your paper. Immediately after you use a direct quote or paraphrase the thought of someone else, you must give credit to the source—including the exact page reference.

If your professor tells you to use Chicago style, you generally either use footnotes or endnotes. A superscript number is inserted at the end of the passage you want to cite. Then you either include a citation as a footnote at the bottom of the page or collect all your citations together as endnotes, at the end of the paper. Unlike bibliography citations, these are more specific, citing the exact page numbers. When using APA or MLA style you don't use footnotes or endnotes; instead you use parenthetical citations. For example, if you quote what Dr. Smith wrote on page two of his book, you just insert (Smith 2) after the quote. The *Chicago Manual of Style* also contains a chapter on author-date citation (Chapter 16), but it is intended more for authors who are writing books than for students doing research papers. Following are some general guidelines on how to cite the main categories of material (books, periodical articles, and Web pages) using the Chicago style, which is the style most commonly used by undergraduates.

CITING BOOKS

The basic components of a book citation are the author, the title, the publisher, and the place and date of publication. For example, here is a typical citation for a book:

> Friedman, Thomas L. *The World Is Flat: A Brief History of the Twenty-First Century.* New York: Farrar, Straus, and Giroux, 2005.

Suppose that within your paper, you also specifically quoted something written on page 95 of Friedman's book. Following Chicago style, you have to provide a footnote or endnote, and it has a slightly different format from the bibliographic citation above:

> [1]Thomas L. Friedman, *The World Is Flat: A Brief History of the Twenty-First Century* (New York: Farrar, Straus, and Giroux, 2005), 95.

Notice that the author's name is not inverted and that the citation is indented. There are also subtle (and annoying) differences in punctuation—commas instead of periods and parentheses around the publisher and date.

If you cite the same source more than once in your paper, Chicago style gets a little easier. Let's say that the footnote immediately following the one above cites something Friedman said on page 143. There is no need to repeat the entire citation; you would just use 'Ibid., 143.' In case you're curious, 'ibid.' stands for 'ibidem,' which in Latin means 'in the same place.' If there were an intervening footnote, however, you would have to use a shortened citation, omitting the subtitle and all but the most essential information: 'Friedman, *The World Is Flat*, 143.'

There are many variations for citing books: your book may have two, three, or more authors, or it may have no author but an editor instead, as in the case of many reference works. It could be a multivolume work or a specific edition. In each of these cases, the citation is a little different, so refer to the style manuals for guidance.

CITING PERIODICAL ARTICLES

By now you should be familiar with the basic components of a periodical article citation, since they are included in all indexes: the author, the title of the article, the title of the periodical in which the article is published, the date of the issue, the page numbers, and, in the case of a journal, the volume and issue numbers.

The format for your citations, however, is a bit different from what you've seen in indexes. Here are a sample bibliographic citation and footnote for an article in a popular magazine:

Loria, Leonard. "Disney without the Mouse." *Yankee*, April 2005, 128–133.

[1]Leonard Loria, "Disney without the Mouse," *Yankee*, April 2005, 130.

If you are citing an article from a scholarly journal, you must also include the volume and issue numbers before the date and page numbers, so the format would follow the example below:

Wright, Chris. "Natural and Social Order at Walt Disney World." *Sociological Review* 54, no. 2 (2006): 303–317.

[1]Chris Wright, "Natural and Social Order at Walt Disney World," *Sociological Review* 54, no. 2 (2006): 310.

If you got the text of an article online, perhaps through InfoTrac or EBSCOhost, the citation format has to reflect this. Let's say you found the *Yankee* article by Leonard Loria online on EBSCOhost's Academic Search Premier. Here's how you would cite it using Chicago style:

Loria, Leonard. "Disney without the Mouse." *Yankee*, April 2005, 128–133. Available from Academic Search Premier [online database] (Boston, Mass.: EBSCO Publishing) <http://search.epnet.com> (25 August 2006).

The rules regarding electronic citation are not set in stone like those for more traditional resources. Refer to the most recent edition of the style guides for more specific instructions. Some of the online databases have help screens that explain how to cite the material contained in them. Be careful, however, because this information is sometimes incorrect. In addition to the citation of the original print source of the article, you must indicate what online service you used, the location and name of the company that produces it, the Web address of the service's homepage, and the date you accessed it. Page numbers are irrelevant when it comes to Web versions of articles, but a citation for the online version of an article that originally appeared in print should indicate the numbers for the print version. If the exact range of pages is not known, just give the first page followed by a plus sign.

CITING WEB SITES

The rules for citing Web pages are similar to those for citing electronic versions of print articles. If you recall that one of the fundamental purposes of citing resources is so others can find them, then the information you should include makes sense. Although the rules are still under development, some general guidelines can be given here. The Web site Online!: A Reference Guide to Using Internet Sources includes a page that interprets Chicago style for online citations. Using the rules provided there, here are the citations for this resource:

> Harnack, Andrew, and Eugene Kleppinger. "Using Chicago Style to Cite and Document Sources." Online!: A Reference Guide to Using Internet Sources. 2003. <http://www.bedfordstmartins.com/online/cite7.html> (25 August 2006).

> [1]Andrew Harnack and Eugene Kleppinger, "Using Chicago Style to Cite and Document Sources," Online!: A Reference Guide to Using Internet Sources, 2003, <http://www.bedfordstmartins.com/online/cite7.html> (23 July 2006).

Other sites agree with this basic structure, advising that the following information be included in citations:

- Author's name—basically, whoever is responsible for the content; this could be an individual or an organization. If no author is indicated, you'll just have to leave it out.
- Title of the Web page and Web site—to understand the difference, here is an analogy: a Web page is like a chapter in a book, while a Web site is like the entire book. In the above example, 'Using Chicago Style to Cite and Document Sources' is the specific Web page, while Online!: A Reference Guide to Using Internet Sources is the name of the entire Web site. Remember a Web page's length is not confined to a certain size as a printed book is.

- Date—when the page was created (or date of most recent update).
- Address—the complete URL (be very careful to double-check; sometimes these can be long).
- Date visited — when you accessed it.

Note that when a periodical is posted on the Web or in an online database you should cite the original publication, rather than the URL of the page on which the article itself is located.

Be sure to document your sources properly—if you don't, you are at risk of plagiarizing. In addition to giving credit to the authors of the sources you used, the purpose of citing sources is to give credibility to the facts you state in your paper, and to enable anyone who reads your paper to locate these sources. Therefore, it is crucial that you include accurate information and double-check all your citations.

A Review of the Research Process

To make sure that you're headed the right way as you finish this book, let's take a look back down the road and review the basic directions for doing effective research:

- Define your topic. You need to know where you're going and what you're looking for. If possible, pick a topic that interests you, just as you would choose a vacation destination for its appeal. Plan your route by determining what types of sources you need, how you will find them, and roughly how much time it will take you. Don't procrastinate!
- Determine what electronic databases are available at your library, then select the most appropriate ones for your topic.
- Search the online catalog for books. If you have problems with subject searching, try keyword searching using the basic principles of Boolean logic. Go to the stacks and locate the books cited in the records you found on the computer. If you need more books, do some "educated browsing" or consider using the collections of other libraries.
- Locate periodical articles on your topic using online indexes, or print indexes for older articles.
- Consult some basic reference sources if you need to check a fact or get some background information.
- If you find too much information when searching a database, narrow your search. If you don't find enough information, broaden your search utilizing the principles outlined in Chapter 2.
- Search the Web. If you have acquired a knowledge of your topic from books and articles, you will be better able to evaluate the accuracy of Web resources. Remember, there's a lot of junk out there. The most effective way to find what you need on the Web is to use search engines, particularly the advanced search screens.

Research is not a linear process like getting from point A to point B. You may find that you have to backtrack and repeat some of the steps listed above. That's okay. You'll ultimately reach your destination if you just keep going.

EPILOGUE

You've traveled a long road since the beginning of this book, and along the way you've been given many directions. With this background, you should feel prepared to take the wheel confidently and travel through the library—both real and virtual.

If you're lost on the road, don't wander around too long before you stop to ask for directions. You can save a lot of time and frustration if you simply ask someone for help. In the same way, you should not hesitate to ask for help in your library. Even after reading this book you may sometimes feel a bit lost. That's understandable, and that's why every library has a reference desk where you can go to find your way amid all the resources available.

On a road trip, you may travel hundreds, even thousands of miles for days, maybe weeks. You might think you've covered a lot of territory, but if you take a look at a globe, you'll realize how little of the world you've actually seen. Even if you spend your lifetime traveling you'll never see it all.

It's the same with information. Consider, for example, that approximately 50,000 books are published each year in the United States alone. Over 10,000 magazines and journals are currently in print. There are *billions* of Web pages! Walking into even an average-sized library and looking at all the books on the shelves can be overwhelming. Just as you will never be able to explore every nook and cranny on Earth, you will never be able to absorb all the accumulated knowledge of the human race.

The important thing is to be able to pinpoint the specific information that addresses your needs. Having read this book, you will now be able to do this more efficiently, saving yourself lots of time and frustration so that you can more fully enjoy your time at college. If you get your research done more efficiently, as you should using the techniques described in this book, reward yourself for a job well done by taking a real road trip during your next break.

Bon voyage!

EXERCISES

1) Using Chicago style, write down the bibliographic citation for one of the books you have located for your current paper topic.

———————————————————

———————————————————

2) Using Chicago style, write down the bibliographic citation for one of the periodical articles you have located for your current paper topic.

———————————————————

———————————————————

3) Using Chicago style, write down the bibliographic citation for one of the Web sites you have located for your current paper topic.

———————————————————

———————————————————

4) Circle the mistakes in each one of the following footnotes.

a) Houchang E. Chehabi. "The Politics of Football in Iran." *Soccer and Society* 7, no. 2/3 (2006): 261.

b) Hewitt, Bill, "MySpace Nation: The Controversy," *People*, 6 July 2006, 113.

c) Marc Siegel, "Bird Flu: Everything You Need to Know about the Next Pandemic" (Hoboken, N.J.: Wiley, 2006), 103.

Answers: 4a) periods are incorrect after author and article title because commas are used in footnotes; 4b) author's name is incorrect because it should not be inverted; 4c) book title in quotation marks is incorrect because it should be in italics.

Index